Perfect victims

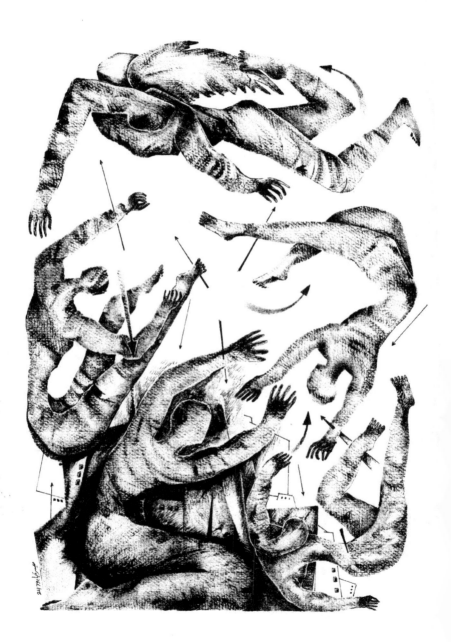

PERFECT VICTIMS

and the Politics of Appeal

MOHAMMED EL-KURD

Haymarket Books
Chicago, Illinois

© 2025 Mohammed El-Kurd

Published in 2025 by
Haymarket Books
P.O. Box 180165
Chicago, IL 60618
www.haymarketbooks.org

ISBN: 979-8-88890-317-9

Distributed to the trade in the US through Consortium Book Sales
and Distribution (www.cbsd.com) and internationally through Ingram
Publisher Services International (www.ingramcontent.com).

This book was published with the generous support of Lannan
Foundation, Wallace Action Fund, and Marguerite Casey Foundation.

Special discounts are available for bulk purchases by organizations
and institutions. Please email info@haymarketbooks.org for more
information.

Cover artwork and frontispiece, *The fall has fallen, and you rise*
(acrylic and ink on Canson paper, 52 x 37.5 cm) © 2024 by Maisara
Baroud.

Printed in the United States.

Library of Congress Cataloging-in-Publication data is available.

For Omar,
who, at the time of writing this,
remains incarcerated in a Zionist prison

In loving memory of
Dr. Refaat al-Areer,
and all those who dared to raise the ceiling

even if!

even if!

even if!

contents

	author's note(s)	1
one	***the sniper's hands are clean of blood*** *on dehumanization*	7
two	***the politics of defanging*** *on "humanization"*	33
three	***shireen's passport*** *on the invention of the civilian*	51
four	***a life in cross-examination*** *on forbidden sentiments*	77
five	***tropes and drones*** *on discursive land mines*	97
six	***mein kampf** in the playroom* *on propaganda*	111
seven	***miraculous epiphanies*** *on testimony*	125
eight	***are we indeed all palestinians?*** *on identity*	171
nine	***"do you want to throw israelis into the sea?"*** *on irreverence*	193
epilogue	***rain is coming***	211
	acknowledgments	215
	works cited	219
	notes	229
	index	240

author's note(s)

1. I have said too much and too little about the subject of this work, which is, even beyond the Palestinian question, a subject referred to by many names and already discussed at great length. This book is my humble attempt at presenting my argument coherently and comprehensively, though it remains, for all intents and purposes, an incomplete work. It is not only grief that makes writing in the time of genocide a torturous task; it is, more so, one's recognition of the written word as shamefully insufficient in the face of 2,000-pound bombs.

2. Our history's bloodiest chapter, one must admit, has accentuated a morbid correlation that has long existed: the more martyrs there are, the more podiums. There is no denying that the Palestinian in the West and many parts of the Arab world confronts staggering levels of violence, suppression, and erasure. However, within certain progressive niches in media, culture, academia, and politics, "Palestine" is emerging as a social currency for certain individuals. One's responsibility here, and the least that anyone can do, is to raise the ceiling of what is permissible.

PERFECT VICTIMS

3. No assessment of a "politics of appeal" can be written without first recognizing that today's world is unlike yesterday's. Our people have sacrificed and struggled artfully to work within and around an unworkable system. While I may often complain about the discursive nature of our battles, I cannot forget that not very long ago we barely existed in any mainstream discourse. It is tempting to continue this thought by saying our civil society infrastructure today dwarfs that of the past, that our late revolutionaries and intellectuals were surveilled, silenced, and suppressed with a brutality that has since fallen out of favor. But Gaza nullifies such a reading. I do not want us to compare our past to our present. I want us to invent a new future, to break out of the hamster wheel.

4. Criticism is good. By this I do not mean self-flagellation or victim blaming; good-faith criticism should be engaged with in good faith. However, I do not consider *Perfect Victims* to be a critique, per se. Nor is it a manifesto, or a monograph. Rather, it is an interrogation of strategies and tactics, ideologies and impulses, and hypotheses and beliefs, an infiltration of the dominant discourses. I try to inject the local and its epistemic authority, which are massively overlooked, into the global—the arrogant, autocratic global. These days, it is fashionable to call this moment in time "unprecedented," but more than that it is existential. The people whose lives are in peril whose willing (and more often unwilling) sacrifices, and whose knowledge production, eloquent or otherwise, continue to shape this

AUTHOR'S NOTE(S)   3

moment will be discounted as protagonists and instead treated as mere anthropological sites of misery, subjection, or past-due epiphanies. I try with this book to resituate those crushed and invisibilized classes, to which I am loyal, as history makers as opposed to historicized objects. But beyond trying to bridge the chasm between Palestine and the world, I want to tackle the tension between the homeland and the diaspora.

5. The word "illegal" does not appear in this manuscript, nor do I rely much on a rights-based framework. Having been born and raised in Palestine, I did not need to be particularly astute to understand the law as often the most lethal weapon in the oppressor's arsenal. While I admire the extraordinary efforts made in that field (vis-à-vis human rights lawyers, South Africa's genocide case at the International Court of Justice, etc.), I do not believe it to be the only language through which we advance the Palestinian cause. There are many books about the law already. And there are vast universes outside of the courthouse.

6. In the first chapters of this book, the reader will notice that the names of Palestinian (or Arab) figures, prisoners, and martyrs are accompanied by short biographies or obituaries in the main body of text; however, as the chapters progress, those identifiers are moved to footnotes. This is not to indicate that their stories are marginal. On the contrary, I want to treat our martyrs and prisoners as household names. I do

4 PERFECT VICTIMS

not want to audition before the reader; I want to address the reader as if they are a guest in *my* living room. I should also mention that the tonal shifts throughout the book (lyricism to analysis, sorrow, sarcasm, indignation, and vice versa) also reflect that intimacy and sovereignty of this kind of narration, which addresses the reader not as a judge but as a curious stranger or better yet a familiar visitor, without fear, jargon, or pretenses.

7. Such shifts, both measured and spontaneous (between Arabic and English, poetry and prose, journalism and political activism, personal narrative and reportage, etc.), also influence the way the text fluctuates, seemingly haphazardly, between first, second, and third person when discussing Palestinians. Sometimes I use "they" to refer to the Palestinian People, as if they are on a faraway planet; other times I say "we" or "I." The different pronoun usage is in fact quite representative of the disparate Palestinian conditions, whether political, socioeconomic, or relational, conditions that are violently marked by colonial fragmentation.

8. Finally, throughout the book, there is a disproportionate use of masculine pronouns. That is done on purpose. For far too long the Palestinians have been reduced to "women and children." One implication here is robbing women and children of their agency and their political or revolutionary contributions. Another is the further demonization of Palestinian men as deserving of death and unworthy of mourn-

ing, exiled from their loved ones' embrace. I often use "he" in reference to "the Palestinian" because I want to force the reader to come face to face with the Palestinian man. I want the reader to contend with that complex and contradictory demographic, and not just those assumed to be the gentle or generous among us—not only the fathers, but the fighters as well.

▼

1. *the sniper's hands are clean of blood*

And the men are men and the women are men
And the children are men!

—Padraic Fiacc[1]

WE DIE A LOT. We die in fleeting headlines, in between breaths. Our death is so quotidian that journalists report it as though they're reporting the weather: *Cloudy skies, light showers, and 3,000 Palestinians dead in the past ten days.* And much like the weather, only God is responsible—not armed settlers, not targeted drone strikes.

We pay no heed to corpses in our fields. Their existence is monotonous, predictable. The slaughter is so relentless, it is almost expected—anticipated—by the soon-to-be-slain. Their wrists, big and tiny, bound with zip ties in the back of police cars. Death is everywhere. Even metaphor is a casualty of war. The figurative has become painfully literal: bloodied beards, furniture in trees, a limb hanging from a ceiling fan, women giving birth on the concrete. Etcetera. Are we too acquainted with the horrific? What was once horrifying, what was once a harbinger of doom, now blends into the terrain; death is now

8   PERFECT VICTIMS

a boring scarecrow. Even when the ravens grow louder, their croaking falls on disinterested ears. No sanctity is left in this death. No deities come to the rescue. We die forsaken. We die a lot in abandonment.

Our massacres are only interrupted by commercial breaks. Judges legalize them. Correspondents kill us with passive voice. If we are lucky, diplomats say that our death concerns them, but they never mention the culprit, let alone condemn the culprit. Politicians, inert, inept, or complicit, fund our demise, then feign sympathy, if any. Academics stand idle. That is, until the dust settles, then they will write books about what should have been. Coin terms and such. Lecture in the past tense. And the vultures, even in our midst, will tour museums glorifying, romanticizing what they once condemned, what they did not deign to defend—our resistance—mystifying it, depoliticizing it, commercializing it. The vultures will make sculptures out of our flesh.[2]

And we die. Snipers here, warplanes there, expulsions, exiles, erasure, genocide, infanticide, humiliation, heartache, bereavement, imprisonment, theft, thirst,* torture, famine, poverty, isolation, defeatism, blackmail, sacrifice, heroism, altruistic suicide. You name it. Our people decompose in the courtyards of hospi-

---

* "Through persistent, systematic, and widespread targeting of the Gaza Strip's water sources and desalination plants, Israel is using water as a weapon against Palestinian civilians. In addition to imposing famine, Israel is deliberately reducing the amount of water available to residents of the Strip." See Euro-Mediterranean Human Rights Monitor, "Israel Uses Water as Weapon."

THE SNIPER'S HANDS ARE CLEAN OF BLOOD   9

tals, like their grandparents who decayed on the Tantura beach. And we die without farewell: What do you say to the families of the martyrs who are occupied even in death? Their children are held hostage in the cemeteries of numbers or frozen in mortuary chambers. Their bodies become bargaining chips.* Or harvested for organs.†

How do you break the news of what should be fictional? Our journalists are poets, almost, when narrating all this death. And the poets write with knives.‡ Our blacksmiths do not make swords, and the rifles in our towns are only for

---

* See Wahbe, "Politics of Karameh"; Hassan, "Warmth of Our Sons." Or see Makaber al-Arqam (مقابر الأرقام), the popular national campaign launched to pressure the Israeli authorities to release the bodies of Palestinian and Arab victims of the Occupation withheld at the Cemetery of Numbers and other morgues, in order for their family members and loved ones to pay them their last respects.

† Euro-Mediterranean Human Rights Monitor has reported "concerns" that the Israeli regime has stolen organs from Palestinian corpses, citing medical professionals who have documented evidence of "possible organ theft by the Israeli military," which includes "missing cochleas and corneas as well as other vital organs like livers, kidneys, and hearts" from bodies of dead Palestinians returned by the Israeli military to southern Gaza. See also *New Arab*, "Israel Harvesting Organs"; Black, "Doctor Admits Israeli Pathologists."

‡ Qabbani, "Footnotes to the Book of the Setback," stanza 3:
> My grieved country,
> In a flash
> You changed me from a poet who wrote love poems
> To a poet who writes with a knife.

"يا وطني الحزين

حولتني بلحظةٍ

من شاعرٍ يكتب الحب والحنين

لشاعرٍ يكتب بالسكين"

guarding the president's mansion. So the youth take to the streets with toy guns. They take on dragons and dinosaurs, the colonizers and their subcontractors. Those born and raised in violence, those who spend their lifetimes staring down the barrels of American-made M4s and M16s, understand they will be massacred whether or not they pick up the Carlo.* We die a lot in stubborn refusal.

---

* A low-cost, improvised submachine gun produced in makeshift workshops in occupied Palestine. Though easy to manufacture, it is inaccurate and prone to jamming and misfire. It is named after the Carl Gustaf M/45.

ZIONISM* IS THE LEADING CAUSE OF DEATH IN OCCU-PIED PALESTINE, through both direct, state-sanctioned violence and indirect, consequential violence, which trickles down through suffocating bureaucracies, inescapable psychological onslaughts, and impetuous intercommunal conflicts. Yet this man-made quietus is treated like any other leading cause of death—heart disease in the US, dementia in England—and is scarcely cause for concern, let alone condemnation. On the contrary, our death is sustenance for the world we live in, necessary to maintain things as they are. Our blood is the price of the colony's sense of "security." The empire cuts the lives of our loved ones short to prolong its reign. And our grief is negligible, our rage unwarranted. The more our loved ones are killed by Zionist colonialism, the less space we are offered to grieve them. We cannot narrate this colossal theft of life, let alone avenge it.

For our martyrs to matter, they need to have lived as spectacular people or endured a spectacularly violent death. And when I say "a spectacularly violent death," I think of the killing of Mohammed Abu Khdeir, a sixteen-year-old boy who was kidnapped by Jewish settlers from his neighborhood in occupied Jerusalem, brutally beaten, forced to drink gasoline,[3] then burned alive.[4] I think of six-year-old Hind Rajab, who was found

---

* Zionism—the political ideology, born in nineteenth-century Central and Eastern Europe, that argued that the creation of a Jewish state would be the only viable solution to the persecution of Jews—is an ideology of dispossession, an expansionist and racist settler-colonial enterprise. The Nakba, enduring and ongoing, remains the clearest crystallization of the Zionist ideology.

murdered by Israeli soldiers alongside the paramedics sent to rescue her[5] twelve days after she called emergency dispatchers from a bullet-riddled car, surrounded by her family's dead bodies,[6] pleading on the phone for three hours, "Come take me. You will come and take me?"[7] I think of the ghoulish and perverse. Otherwise, as in most cases, after the news breaks in silence, our martyrs' loved ones join a long line of families who lament away from cameras and only know to ask God for justice. Otherwise, as in most cases, the slain are condemned to become another forgotten statistic, or even deserving of death.

Israeli death, on the other hand, is another story, the main story. The love their dead receive is fiery, ardent, incandescent—it lights up the White House and Eiffel Tower. The globe grieves Israeli loss without qualifiers and morphs that grief into fuel for genocide. Here, grief becomes a currency. Here, love becomes a guise. "And among the lovers is one who masters the conscience / and another who claims coalescing [in that mastery] / Even if the tears on their cheeks look alike / It is palpable who wept and who feigned weeping."[8]*

Two days after October 7th's Hamas offensive on the Israeli colonies encircling Gaza, the Palestinian Authority's ambassador to the UK (a political opponent of Hamas) gave an interview to the BBC, just hours after six of his family members had fallen victim to an Israeli airstrike. "They were simply bombarded. Their entire building was brought down," he told the host.[9] His

---

* "وَفي الأَحبابِ مُختَصٌّ بِوَجدٍ — وَآخَرُ يَدَّعي مَعَهُ اشتِراكا
إذا اشتَبَهَت دُموعٌ في خُدودٍ — تَبَيَّنَ مَن بَكى مِمَّن تَباكى"

family members were among the thousands (now tens of thousands, if not hundreds of thousands) killed in the ongoing genocidal assault on the tiny, densely populated strip, where more than two million live besieged.

"My cousin Ayah, her two children, her husband, her mother-in-law, and two other relatives died immediately, were killed instantly, and two of their youngest children, a twin, two years old, are now in intensive care," he said.

The host replied, "Sorry for your own personal loss. I mean, can I just be clear, though, you cannot condone the killing of civilians in Israel, can you?"[10]

Such responses to our terrible losses, whether on the international stage or in the media, are not merely callous. They reveal a far more troubling truth: the standard, across industries, is to dehumanize the Palestinian.[11]

WHEN I SPEAK OF DEHUMANIZATION, I do not mean, at least not exclusively, the movies where actors paint their faces brown and scream *Allahu Akbar* or the moments of televised fury when politicians slip up and call us "human animals."[12] Nor do I mean the unmistakably racist rhetoric that animalizes us, that says we have "swarmed" here and "infested" there, that we are "hordes" of savages and beasts. After all, as a poet, I am also guilty of aestheticizing my work with bestiaries.

Dehumanization is not merely the sentiment—arrogance? ignorance? fear?—that compels columnists and envoys illiterate in Arabic to write smug reports (libelous diatribes, really) on "the region." When I speak of dehumanization, I am referring to a phenomenon more implicit, yet far more pernicious and institutionalized, a practice perfected by our politest murderers. When I speak of dehumanization, I am referring to the West's refusal to look us in the eye.

It is the world's reluctance or incapacity to see our tragedies as tragedies and our reactions as reactions, its insistence on categorizing our normalities as deviance. Fundamental instincts—e.g., survival, self-defense—and the basic conduct intrinsic to life on earth become luxuries only they can indulge. The dehumanizers are not only the vulgar right-wingers and the brutal policemen but the most politically correct of killers who deny us even eye contact before they pull the trigger, sniping coldly, impersonally, from hundreds of meters away. The sniper here, the removed figure with the authority to erase our existence without ever having to engage it, endures in both a literal sense, on our hilltops and rooftops, and a metaphorical sense, in governments and in newsrooms. In this reality, the sniper's hands are clean of blood.

And the snipers are everywhere: the underhanded journalists, the spineless bureaucrats, the inconspicuous henchmen, the philanthropists who mine our tragedies for gold, the television anchors who obfuscate those tragedies, the missionaries who find their salvation in our demise, the devil's advocates, the distractors, those who litter our roads with red herrings, the unscrupulous political advisors, the activists who act as puppet masters, the elite capturers, the elitists in our ranks who demand of us a certain dance, who imprison us in the panopticon of their gaze, the self-appointed intellectuals, the clergy who whisper when they should scream, the very well-fed weapons manufacturers and the university administrators who feed them, and the academics indulging in arrogance and willful misinterpretation, who mutilate Frantz Fanon and Walter Benjamin, deny human nature, and contest even the laws of physics in order to pathologize our resistance. In this reality, the sniper's hands are clean of blood, but his body count is insurmountable.

Dehumanization has situated us—ejected us, even—outside of the human condition, so much so that what is logically understood to be a man's natural reaction to subjugation is an uncontained and incomprehensible, primal behavior if it comes from us. What makes some people heroes is what makes us criminals. It is almost simplistic to say that we are guilty by birth. Our existence is purely mechanistic; we are reminded, through policy and procedure, that we are unfortunately born to die. And in our deterministic march to the grave, we encounter each other as unlucky strangers, fledgling and futureless. Our intellectual contributions and institutional participation are restrained. No attribute shall apply to the Palestinian People ("the Palestinians," as they call us) except the damning or the passive. We are not human beings, we are enigmas, infuriating, frightening enigmas, whose every action invites indictment and whose every sentiment is an embryonic threat.

THE SNIPER'S HANDS ARE CLEAN OF BLOOD 17

WHEN TELEVISION PRODUCERS INVITE US to participate in their programs, they do not seek to interview us for our experiences or analysis or the context we can provide. They do not offer us their condolences the way they do our Israeli counterparts. They invite us to interrogate us. The former director general of the Israeli Ministry of Strategic Affairs* called it "waging a holistic campaign against the other side. Take him out of his comfort zone. Make him be on the defensive."[13] *Argumentum ad hominem.* "You discredit the messenger as a way of discrediting the message" has long been an Israeli mantra.[14] For our plight cannot be "discredited," but our characters can be. They turn us into criminals of thought, guilty of our rage and grudges, of our natural responses to brutalization. They test our answers against the viewer's inherent bias. The bombs raining down on the besieged Gaza Strip become secondary, if not entirely irrelevant, to our televised trials. We die a lot as defendants.

How we have been perceived, engaged, and governed, for centuries, in and by the West is dictated by our status as "brutes." Even when that status is no longer explicitly codified into law, that is, if one believes that humanity is defined by citizenry, it still lingers. It hides in the fine print. Though Aboriginal and Torres Strait Islanders gained the status of British subjects under the 1920 Nationality Act (well, only those of them born in and after 1921) and were automatically assigned Australian citizenship under the

---

* Her name is Sima Vaknin-Gil. The Ministry of Strategic Affairs is now part of the Ministry of Foreign Affairs.

18 PERFECT VICTIMS

1948 Nationality and Citizenship Act, they could not marry without the consent of the Australian authorities, nor could they leave the country without the permission of the immigration minister until 1973.[15] They were not included in the population count until the 1971 census.* To this day, they continue to face colonial violence and erasure. Citizenship has historically been a hollow formality for those condemned to the category of the dehumanized.

Palestinians, regardless of their legal status, and often because of their legal status, are told to despise themselves from the moment they begin observing their environment. We are nowhere in the atlas, our enemies gloat, and barely in the official archives. Our world is built by the settler, for the settler. ("Settler" feels like too soft a word, too forgiving; "homicidal burglar" is more apt). The settler holds the gavel, the baton, and boasts a divine decree. The settler controls our groundwater, seas, and rain, and bills us for them, even criminalizes our thirst. After drawing the borders, he now dominates the borders. He controls our roads and what passes through them. He can, and does, clog the arteries of our nation.

---

* Following the 1967 Australian Aboriginals Referendum.

ONE'S FIRST ENCOUNTER WITH THE CRUEL REAL-
ITY OF COLONIZATION is unforgettable and irreversible. I
was five or six years old as I watched my mother, inexplicably at
the time, try to outwit the settler by smuggling meat under her
passenger seat as my father drove back to Jerusalem from Bethlehem. I did not understand what made our groceries contraband.
Or why we needed to pass through a military barrier. Or why my
father drove with his blue ID card between his index and middle
finger. I did not know why his ID was blue when my aunt's was
green. Or why the soldiers hassled us for hours and searched,
even in our intentions, for reasons to put us in handcuffs.

Long before I understood, or even noticed, this power imbalance between the colonizer and the colonized, I recognized that
something about my presence was irreconcilable, that I could
not merely exist without a bespoke explanation that justifies my
being, a narrative of sorts. Every neighbor had a narrative, every
classmate. Some of us were internally displaced, others eternally
impoverished. Our narratives were rationalizations, really, for
our place in the world, or lack thereof—our place, in every sense
of the word.

The consequences of dehumanization, the staggering and
the subtle, reveal themselves not only in how we are perceived
but in how we perceive ourselves. They are intrapersonal and
intracommunal. Intimate trespasses. The brutality of the dehu-
manizer has followed us even into our living rooms, shaping
how we self-conceptualize, how we raise our children and build
our institutions. It has infested newsrooms and campuses. It
has invaded our places of worship. Ruined our hospitals. And it

has filled our hearts with fear, a vigilant, rehearsed fear that has turned thunderous declarations into anonymous whispers.

Throughout my childhood, I observed those around me— my parents in our home, the Old City's sellers of ceramics and souvenirs, tour guides and taxi drivers—recite seemingly memorized preludes to their statements, as if to preempt an anticipated accusation. None of this was in our mother tongue. This was an arduous sport we played outside of Arabic, when *el ajanib*, "the foreigners," would grace us with their presence. An *ajnabi* could mean anyone: the visiting diplomat, the prying activist, the perverted tourist, the Long Island fraudster,* the "wanderers in the waste land."[16] Anyone illiterate in our unspoken language of nods and smirks or, worse, anyone suspicious of it. Always on the defense, we define ourselves by what we are *not*, not what we are. It is this condition, living and blaring, that the Palestinian is born to reverse.

---

* "And if I don't steal it, someone else is gonna steal it."

THE SNIPER'S HANDS ARE CLEAN OF BLOOD   21

HERE IN THE WEST (WHATEVER "THE WEST" MEANS THESE DAYS), whether on television screens, university campuses, in public office, or in the public's imagination, Palestinians exist in a false—and strict—dichotomy: we are either victims or terrorists.

Those who are deemed terrorists never get the opportunity to speak for themselves and are rarely offered due diligence, if at all.* They are almost mythical creatures, the stuff of scary stories: big bad wolves with furrowed, hairy eyebrows, sharp fangs, and terrifyingly incorrect politics. They roam the streets mumbling in aggressive Arabic, sometimes even reading the Quran, salivating to loot and shoot everything in sight. Beware—they're coming after you. Hide your wives, hide your planes, hide your human shields. Many who are reading these sentences have a mental image of whom I am describing and, it wouldn't be far-fetched to say, associate serious feelings and memories with such mental images. Those of us who are deemed terrorists cannot be grieved.

On the other hand, those who are victims, or granted the victim status even after they failed to die, are sometimes given the microphone and asked to speak. But their articulations

---

* In public discourse, the criteria for what makes someone a terrorist are loose. Terrorism, above all (and this is not an especially sharp assessment), is about one's political motivations, not one's actions. It is about one's race, religion, and rhetoric. This is particularly true in the Israeli judiciary. For example, in 2021, the Israeli regime designated six leading Palestinian civil society and human rights groups as "terror organizations," including, comically, Defense for Children International. See El-Kurd, "New Campaign."

on said mic come at a steep price. There are prerequisites they must meet. Palestinian victims must be wounded and weak: too wounded to fight and too weak to frown or furrow their eyebrows. And if they are bereaved, they can only be the wailing widows whose grief is too inexplicable to contextualize, the orphans whose slain parents' obituaries omit "cause of death." Their anguished cries exist outside of history and politics, their injuries are reported without a culprit.

If the invitation to speak is extended to Palestinians who were once wolves, they are now docile and defanged, only howling at the moon in agony.* They never charge or attack, let alone hunt in a pack. If they advocate for themselves, they must narrate only their personal tragedies. Neither political ideology nor, God forbid, nationalist ambitions should ever incentivize their campaigning. It must remain individualistic, never for a collective cause and never through an organized collective, and must solely seek to remedy humanitarian crises that, like earthquakes and eclipses, occur in isolation from the global state of affairs.

Our response to this dichotomy—rather, our response to being charged with terrorism, to being ejected outside of the human condition—has been a politics of appeal, a practice that utilizes a set of creative advocacy tactics designed to advance our cause, ceaselessly attempting to fulfill the aforementioned

---

* One of my friends insisted that I clarify that it is in fact a myth that wolves howl at the moon at all. Wolves howl as a social rallying cry, to initiate a hunt, express territorial dominance, or to alert other wolves of their location.

requirements. Once the criteria are conquered, magically, marvelously, the Palestinian can finally escape the circumscribed category of the terrorist and find refuge in the even narrower node of victimhood.[17]

24 PERFECT VICTIMS

*Put your head between these heads
and call on the beheader.*

—Levantine proverb*

THE THIEF HOLDS A GAVEL; the liar holds a journalism degree; and the butcher's knives are publicly funded. People who engage in a politics of appeal recognize, sometimes begrudgingly, often without much protest, that our world is ruled by hierarchies and emperors that do not favor us whatsoever. That the world is upside down is an easy truth, accepted by most. That everyday people can change the world is an improbable scenario. Power, in this analysis, is an immutable, indelible structure set in stone, rather than an imposing yet tenuous entity resting on sand. Hardened, fortified, billion-dollar sand, but—*but!*—sand nonetheless.

Through this axiomatic view of power, one can understand a politics of appeal to be, at best, shrewd attempts to outsmart

---

* This proverb (حط راسك بين هالروس وقول يا قطاع الروس) is not in reference to ISIS, as the colonial imagination would suppose, but was in fact a reference to colonial oppression itself, becoming especially popular during the British occupation of Palestine (1917–1948), when the Palestinian peasant, in the words of Ghassan Kanafani, transformed into "a creature of abject fatalism" due to "abject poverty, crushing repression, and centuries of class and national repression." Such conditions created an atmosphere of "defeatism, fatalism, and political quietism that was reflected in the most widespread proverbs and sayings." In Kanafani's analysis, the intellectuals—particularly the poets—worked to overturn this culture of quietism into a culture of resistance, where anticolonial courage was embraced where once it was feared. See Kanafani, *Revolution of 1936–1939 in Palestine*, 26–27.

THE SNIPER'S HANDS ARE CLEAN OF BLOOD 25

the system, to beat it at its own game. Or, at worst, it can be read through a strictly reformist lens: an effort to alter the status quo, never to demolish it altogether. In the case of the latter, those who pledge allegiance to this status quo likely do so because they earnestly believe in the binaries it upholds (good vs. evil, civilized vs. uncivilized, terrorist vs. soldier, etc.) but feel there are certain exceptions to those dichromatic categories. For example, some might respect the violence of men and women in military fatigues as a prosaic, indispensable fact of life, while simultaneously clutching their pearls at violent acts orchestrated by "lone wolves" in flip-flops and tracksuits.*

In placating this worldview, we have unwittingly reinforced the social and institutional order that has created this conundrum for us in the first place. And we have unwittingly reproduced that which we seek to subvert (and should want to abolish). Once we internalize the dichotomy, we produce perfect victims not only for sincere sympathizers and deeply committed allies, but for the entire zealous congregation: the overbearing activists, the voyeuristic liberals, the empathic army wives, the repentant Afrikaners, and the grandchildren of Nazis.

To practice a politics of appeal is to utilize all the tools made available by the institution, "the master's tools," often haplessly, though sometimes with moderate success. And always in line with the institution's logic. Not only have we been taught to

---

* I exclude from this critique those who are ideologically pacifists on principle.

26 PERFECT VICTIMS

"ignore our differences" and indulge "in the pathetic pretense" that they do not exist,* but also to mimic an impossibly congruous, mythical creature—*the innocent civilian*—in hopes to be acquitted of the crime of being Palestinian. Now and then, every once in a while, the judge—*the thief! the burglar!*—might decide an execution is bad optics or that a robbery does not justify the headache. The juice isn't worth the squeeze. Though rare, such a deviance is bound to happen.† However, the day the judge sets the court on fire is the day "the donkey goes up the minaret."‡

But then again we have seen stranger things than a donkey braying the call to prayer. We have seen a nation punished for another nation's genocide. And we have seen God employed as a real-estate agent, bestowing Jerusalem houses to Brooklynites.[18] So nothing is impossible. It might be true then: if we trim our bushy eyebrows and extract our canine teeth, if we pluck the thorny and offensive from our lexicon, if we renounce the Quran and its boisterous Arabic, and if we would only leave those rocks and planes alone, we will be set free. Free to be depicted in documentaries and plastered on newspa-

---

* In *Sister Outsider*, Audre Lorde wrote these words to refer specifically to the demands made of women in Western society, stating: "As women, we have been taught either to ignore our differences, or to view them as causes for separation and suspicion rather than as forces for change."

† "Hundreds of thousands of Palestinians have been tried and convicted in farcical [Israeli military] court proceedings—at a conviction rate of over 99% . . ." See *Eyes on Israeli Military Courts*, Addameer Prisoner Support, 2.

‡ Palestinian proverb, akin to "when pigs fly." (لمّا يطلع الحمار على المئذنة)

pers. Free to be grieved. To speak of Palestine, from Palestine, from Palm Springs, from Prichsenstadt. From podiums and pulpits (never from minbars,* of course). Free to pronounce our Ps at last.

---

* A short flight of steps used as a platform by a preacher in a mosque. (مِنبَر)

28 PERFECT VICTIMS

APPEALING TO THE MORAL SENSE of the people who are oppressing us is not the nucleus of the politics of appeal; rather, it is one facet among others. One that some would argue was once historically necessary. Other tactics include ingratiating oneself with traditional and nontraditional structures of power, exploiting certain social and political phenomena, or appealing to socioeconomic interests. Etcetera. One tactic I find myself using often is reminding US taxpayers that the Zionist regime receives an annual gift of billions of their dollars in the form of military aid. Emphasizing the subordinate clause, that the weapons used to subjugate Palestinians are American-made, is a sad attempt at refocusing the issue or beautifying my rationale: most Americans might not think much of Palestinians, but their money is always on their mind.*

The list of tactics goes on. Appealing to authority, emotion, purity: "Article 49 of the Fourth Geneva Convention says . . ."† "Imagine if this Palestinian kid was *your* child . . ." "No true Jew would support Israel . . ." Intersectionality: highlighting police exchange programs, cyber warfare, climate change, the arms

---

* Since 2021, and especially in 2023, there is no denying that Palestine is on the mind of many Westerners. Mass mobilization for Palestine in the US and West has proven that public opinion on the so-called conflict, Zionism, and Palestinian resistance has shifted positively. The aftermath of such a seismic shift is yet to be felt in its entirety, particularly as it relates to policy, but there is no denying that Palestine is at the center of the stage.

† "Individual or mass forcible transfers, as well as deportations of protected persons from occupied territory to the territory of the Occupying Power or to that of any other country, occupied or not, are prohibited, regardless of their motive."

THE SNIPER'S HANDS ARE CLEAN OF BLOOD   29

trade, "tested on Palestinians, used in Kashmir," "there are Christians in Gaza," and so on. Diplomatic maneuvers: sending delegations of children to speak to politicians, talking about your "Israeli friends" on international platforms, anti-antisemitism disclaimers before every speech, "security coordination," peace accords.

And one should not forget how the politics of appeal has shaped culture- and knowledge-production: for every radical work of literature, there are several more Palestine-related books with children, ragamuffin and smiling, on the cover, no matter the specific topic of the book; for every unabashed, unfiltered film, there are several more desperately persuasive documentaries that border on "trauma porn" and movies whose protagonist is a docile, doe-eyed young girl. Some of these tactics are effective to an impressive degree, others not so much, and all are (almost) always applied sincerely.

In these pages, I will not attempt to assess whether poetry or any other medium can be of use to the Palestinian. I want to examine the Palestinian as he appears in any certain poem (or film, or UN speech, or media interview)—his affect, aim, and motive, the height of his ceiling. How is he presented to the reader? Is he making a cameo in someone else's story line? Is he performing? Does he have words? Does he stand tall? If so, is his strong stature stimulated by societal obligations and external pressure? If not, is his weak stance also a response to these factors? What remains of his "subjectivity," as my dear academics like to say? Does he have his teeth?

The tactics and strategies, or, more frankly, the attitudes that I am mostly interested in and engrossed by are those that rely on "humanization" (or: defanging) and what I will refer to as miraculous epiphanies. The latter, in short, are characterized by an obsessive curation of "reliable narrators," whose testimonies are unthreatening, authoritative, or impartial. To illustrate: favoring Jewish and Israeli sources (books, human rights organizations, rabbis, historians, ex-soldiers, soldiers, cops, government officials, political analysts) over Palestinian sources, not based on the content of their contributions but on an identitarian basis, a choice rooted in the farcical, though deep-seated notion that the former are somehow more credible, more reliable. As if they are unbiased bystanders, as if they have no horse in the race. As for humanization, which I discuss in the following pages, one example is the fine, often mandatory art of making hagiographies for the living and the dead, to manufacture for them a solemn reverence, a remedy to the profanity of their perceived affiliations. Simply put, the perplexing demand to make humans out of humans.

Though these are important political questions, questions that pertain to media analysis, diplomacy, movement building or organizing, I am struck by this conundrum in a more profound, almost philosophical sense, a more "universal" sense. Not universal in a way that indulges the capitalist, commercial connotations of the word, glossing over power, history, and barbed wire, but a universality that recognizes the Palestinian condition *is* the human condition. Palestine is a microcosm of the world: wretched, raging, fraught, and fragmented. On fire. Stubborn. Ineligible. Dignified. The lens we lend the Palestinian reveals how we see each other, how we see everything else.

What is it—power? race? coloniality?* language? class? media? religion? geography? identity? culture? politics? tribalism? behavioral patterns? environment? fear? love? human nature? animal aggression?—What is the profound force, the impetus that incites in our foes and friends alike the refusal to look us in the eye?

▼

---

* PhD word.

2. *the politics of defanging*

> *I love you . . . I mutilate you.*
> —Jacques Lacan[1]

I HAVE ALWAYS WANTED TO BECOME HUMAN. Or, to report more honestly, I have always been advised to want to become human. No manual teaches how to attain this sacred, sought-after status, so, naturally, one mimics. You observe things until you discern a pattern—in school, on television, on propaganda posters. Then you reproduce that pattern—on the page, when speaking to diplomats and reporters, in how you interact with your surroundings, in your internal dialogues.

When I wrote short stories about my grandmother Rifqa as a survivor of the 1948 Nakba, I was told to "humanize" her. I searched in her character for quirks and quips that might pollute her humanity, then I effaced them: the off-color or classist remarks she would mutter about living in an UNRWA* housing

---

* United Nations Relief and Works Agency for Palestine Refugees in the Near East.

project (*May God curse the time that mixed wheat with tares*), the vitriolic descriptions she had assigned the Jewish settlers originally responsible for her statelessness (*Ajoona min kol qaryeh kharyeh*), and her bitter anger toward "the largest armed robbery in modern history,"[‡] which I replaced with a muted "resilience." I cited the tears, never the spit.

You need to be polite in your suffering, should you be granted the right to a roof over your head. Crass statements are corrosive to your plight, even when such statements are about those who first steal your home and then loot your tent. The violence inflicted upon our lands and our bodies, we are told, is secondary to the blemishes tarnishing our image, the blemishes that stand between us and justice, it seems. The smears we live to scrub clean.

---

[*] Palestinian proverb. (الله يلعن هالزمان اللي خلط القمح مع الزوان)
[†] Ask your Arabic-speaking friend to translate.
[‡] In the words of Raeda Taha, Palestinian playwright.

SO WHAT IS HUMANIZATION? An aspirational sensibility? A colonial divide-and-conquer strategy doing the exact opposite of what it purports to do? A malevolent devalorization? An honest effort to counter the anti-Palestinian racism running rampant in the mainstreams of the West? If we think about humanization as a "well-intentioned" project we then can define it through its supposed objectives. Humanization seeks to undo implicit or explicit biases ingrained against "the Palestinians" through depicting us in "respectable" and "relatable" terms, often with an emphasis on individuality or, if a group, the passivity of said collective. Correspondents, cultural workers, our allies, and, of course, we ourselves have long adopted this framework as the foundation of our representational processes: compelling pathos to divorce us from our sullen, menacing stereotype; ethos for credence and credibility; and the exhausting, tedious recitals of facts and statistics in the face of coherently incoherent propaganda. I won't go as far as to call it logos.

It is the ceaseless infantilization of the dehumanized subject. For the spectators to sympathize with "the other," they must first sanitize and subdue him, sever him from his origin story, rendering him "utterly displaced and effaced."[2] We sanctify our victims in our testimonials and eulogies, adorning them with commiserating anecdotes. We hamper them with innocence. And we do this not only in the Palestinian context but also with regard to Black American victims of police brutality: "They were artists" or "They were mentally ill" or "They were unarmed."[3] (It is as if condemning the state for sanctioning the

36   PERFECT VICTIMS

death of a Black person is permissible only if the slain person is a sterile model of American citizenry.) One could say the same about sexual assault victims: we must notify the listener that the victim was sober and dressed appropriately. And more: we promise those spectating that if they deign to come face to face with the dehumanized, they would see their own reflection in our benign, haggard eyes.

Here, the human is defined as someone who fits neatly into the category of the civilian or someone whose disposition and diction communicate a particular class or someone who is a citizen (of certain countries) or someone perceived to be without political agency or military capability or someone who is exceptional or someone who has endured an exceptionally violent fate or someone whose belief system aligns with or poses no danger to the ruling class; or someone who has not inherited their grandfather's rejectionism, their father's dislike for peace, or the munition factory in their mother's womb.

So we flaunt an EU passport like a piece of exonerating evidence. And we cite the honorable professions, waving the press card and the diploma as if they are golden tickets. And the bloodied scrubs. And the stethoscope: sometimes a lifeline, other times a noose. We remind the sniper of the halos on our heads, the crosses we bear, the blindness we heal. Of our other cheek. Of mercy. We don't hate you, we hate the circumstance. We are women and children, always, and if we are men, then we are frail and elderly, reiterating our nonviolence, gesturing at each other's amputated limbs, the branches cut from our trees, more crosses to carry. No land to sow. No sovereignty over the sniper's blooming desert—his dominion "stretch[es] to the height of mountains."[4] We take his jurisprudence as a God and worship in his courthouse.

PERFECT VICTIMS

THE PROBLEM IS, IF YOU WANT TO HUMANIZE the Palestinian, you have to *defang* the Palestinian. The humanity we have been prescribed by the well-intentioned and the malicious alike, or the humanity we have invented for ourselves, follows an intricate, dizzying rule book, its commandments written in hieroglyphics. You learn as you fail that it is ineligible, the project of humanization sustained by perpetual victimhood and regulated through ethnocentric parameters for sympathy and solidarity. In this framework, our affective and psychic allowances are extremely parsimonious. Meaning that humanization, by design, restricts the range of sentiments and emotions we are permitted to express openly, the values, ideologies, and affiliations we can claim without retribution, and even searches in our thoughts and fantasies, in our inferred intentions and ignorances, and in our tacit beliefs for attributes to censor and reeducate.

Our status, too, is scrutinized. Everything is currency and all is calculated: not only the careers we choose and the characteristics we embody but also the legal papers we treasure and our treasures themselves, the class we are born into, the locales and bodies into which we are thrust. We are not human, automatically, by virtue of being human—we are to be *humanized* by virtue of our proximity to innocence: whiteness, civility, wealth, compromise, collaboration, nonalignment, nonviolence, helplessness, futurelessness. This lethal exercise in tightroping is meant to prevent us from falling back into the ring of the condemned.

Humanization diverts critical scrutiny away from the colonizer and onto the colonized, obscuring the inherent injustice

THE POLITICS OF DEFANGING 39

of colonialism, thus shielding the colonial project. In misplacing their focus, advocates (or lawyers or journalists, etc.) insinuate that the oppressed must demonstrate their worthiness of liberty and dignity, first and foremost. Otherwise occupation, subjugation, police brutality, dispossession, surveillance, and "extrajudicial executions," would be excusable or even necessary. The moral code produced within such a framework is rife with logical fallacies and marked by an absence of serious power and material analysis. However implicitly, it accepts the Israeli apparatus, an apparatus of racial and socioeconomic domination, as applicable if need be, rather than an unmistakable example of all that is sordid and deplorable. As such, humanization *pulverizes* the permissible. And it does so in ways that are far more tangible than they are aesthetic or discursive. The majority of the Palestinian People fail to "humanize" themselves, that is, fail to survive dancing on land mines, and the world abandons them. Those of us who are imperfect or are not as lucky. Those of us who will not extract our teeth. Those of us who are "terrorists."

Most people, I think, agree with me, in theory. Some, in fact, would say this argument is self-evident, almost too obvious to write down. Nevertheless, in practice, we remain ensnared by the psychological cues instilled in us by colonial logic. We anticipate the pitfalls that await us in our tracks, as if we have dug them ourselves. We take responsibility for them, we self-reproach. We know the names of the watchdogs that shepherd us into place, the guidelines they bark at us. They are addicted to the fear our bodies exude, and we have been programmed to supply it. We respond like automatons.

40 PERFECT VICTIMS

To illustrate: when the Israeli occupation forces killed fifteen-year-old Adam Ayyad in Dheisheh refugee camp in Bethlehem,* the question was, *Did he really throw a Molotov cocktail at the soldiers? Aren't the Israelis known for fabricating such stories?* When instead the question should have been, *Why are Israeli troops in Bethlehem in the first place? Why was Adam Ayyad born in a refugee camp? Why is "Molotov" in the headline of a story about soldiers killing a boy? So what if he throws a Molotov cocktail? Who wouldn't?*

---

* "Adam Issam Shaker Ayyad, 15, was shot and killed by Israeli forces around 4:30 a.m. on January 3, [2023,] in Dheisheh refugee camp, just outside the city of Bethlehem in the southern occupied West Bank. . . . Israeli forces entered Dheisheh refugee camp earlier that morning to arrest a Palestinian man. Palestinians confronted Israeli forces, who fired live ammunition, rubber-coated metal bullets, sound bombs, and tear gas canisters at the crowds. Adam sustained at least one gunshot wound to the back of his shoulder. He was transferred to Al-Hussein Hospital in nearby Beit Jala in a private car, where doctors pronounced him dead." Defense for Children International - Palestine, "Israeli Forces Kill Two."

SOMETIMES PEOPLE, OFTEN PALESTINIANS, REJECT THIS CRITIQUE OF HUMANIZATION. They view the phenomenon not as an engineered framework, but as a serendipitous congruence: the state where one's conduct and articulations mirror or closely resemble their ideal self. They assert that our march of impeccable virtuousness is not choreographed; we walk like we know how, instinctively. We are not performing a faultless persona, rather we are improvising from the heart. Another version of this argument invokes the language of "moral authority," particularly the belief that by adhering to and embodying high ethical standards and integrity, the oppressed will earn, incrementally, the recognized right to influence the actions and perceptions of others, including their oppressors. "Be good for the good of your cause," the argument goes.

But these claims are blind to their own ethnocentrism: there is no such thing as a universal. Rhetoric, behavior, and one's state of being are contoured by geographic, economic, and sociopolitical idiosyncrasies. This is not a case for Palestinian exceptionalism. On the contrary, I am echoing a basic aphorism: people are different in different places and words mean different things. The word "shahid" (martyr), for example, carries distinct subtexts depending on the context; its connotations are passive and active, encompassing the victimized and the heroic, "whether a member of an Islamic, Christian, secular, or Marxist organization, whether targeted or untargeted."[5] If we want to address the empire, we need to be fluent in its vernacular. But this expectation is asymmetrical. We are often admonished by critics who are illiterate, or purport to be illiterate, in our language. Too frequently, our words and phrases are maligned by dim dilettantes who do not know their definitions to begin with. Or worse, by those who readily obfuscate the regional and historical contexts of specific expressions in order to pathologize them. Their hostile inquisitions do not seek meaning.

Moreover, the discourses surrounding "congruence" and "moral authority" act as though colonialism has not erected barriers of irreconcilability (as well as literal cement barriers) that separate us from humanity. We are dehumanized, thus we are incapable of humanizing ourselves. Appealing to a "moral universality" cannot save us, for there is no room for us within that morality. Zionism's objection to the Palestinian People isn't about *how* we exist but that we exist at all. There is no worldly affect that we can typify into absolution: not a commitment to nonviolence or equanimity, not even postpolitical merit, can dismantle the racial, colonial, and economic barriers on the road to becoming "human." Here in the middle, there is a hungry abyss. We tightrope across the narrow, fragile wire, taking delicate steps.

THE POLITICS OF DEFANGING 43

AND TO TIGHTROPE IS NO EASY TASK. Read the "wrong" book, follow the "wrong" leader, joke inappropriately, invoke a trope, knowingly or unknowingly, show animosity, read about resistance, write about resistance, graffiti the walls, pick up a rifle, and they will kill you. Sometimes even if you wave a white flag.* Our enemy always possesses probable cause. Something as simple and random as your gender is sufficient to fling you far away from humanity. One cannot simply mourn a Palestinian man, not before absolving him first of his cardinal sin, the crime of being Palestinian.

Obituaries of dead Palestinian men deploy certain identifiers (profession, education level, beliefs, and, more recently, sexuality) not to eulogize but to advocate for the deceased, to satisfy the requisite conditions for grieving the deceased. There are prerequisites without which one cannot denounce the actions of the killers. Denouncing the killers themselves is another story.

---

* On December 6, 2023, six members of the Abu Salah family—Inshirah, Saadi, and four of their children: Mahmoud, Ahmad, Yousif, and Srour— were waving a white flag when they were shot dead from close range by Israeli occupation forces in northern Gaza. The Abu Salahs were on their way back from burying their teenage relative, Asaad, who had been shot in the heart with an explosive bullet by an Israeli sniper just hours before. The Israelis then bulldozed their remains into a pile of garbage. Many Palestinians in Gaza have deployed makeshift white flags in hopes of escaping the murderous whims of the occupation forces. In many instances, Palestinians carrying such flags have still been targeted. Even when three Israeli hostages used white flags to identify themselves to occupation forces, they were still shot at. Of course, while the Israeli occupation forces (IOF) does not often admit killing Palestinians waving white flags, it admitted having mistakenly killed the hostages.

PERFECT VICTIMS

After Refaat al-Areer* was murdered alongside several members of his family in a targeted assassination in December 2023, I wrote, in Arabic, that I could not compose a tribute for Refaat in the anglophone news site where I worked as culture editor. To attempt to eulogize a Palestinian man in the colonizer's lexicon is to self-flagellate. They erase their crimes from the archives and erase us from their history books; they create nations with no natives in their dictionaries, nations that pretend not to know whose blood it is on their hands. Announcing one's death requires extracting recognition of one's existence in the first place. English, the language engraved on the missiles that killed Refaat, converts the Palestinian funeral into an arena of strenuous persuasion and pedagogy, where there are no givens or objective facts.

And so, when eulogizing a Palestinian man, we take on the roles of historians, activists, and political analysts, and we riddle our overtures with UN resolutions and human rights reports. The colonizer's language commands that we qualify him for mourning before mourning, that we wash him of his sins—his geography, religion, color, sex, and affiliations—and exclude

---

* Dr. Refaat al-Areer (1979–2023) was a Palestinian writer, poet, and professor from Gaza City. He taught comparative literature and creative writing at the Islamic University of Gaza and cofounded We Are Not Numbers, an organization that mentors young writers from Gaza and promotes storytelling as a tool of Palestinian resistance. He was known for his political analysis and satirical commentary on social media. On December 7, 2023, Refaat was targeted and killed by an Israeli airstrike on the Shejaiya refugee camp in the north of the Gaza Strip.

THE POLITICS OF DEFANGING 45

him from the ranks of our fighters and fight to exhibit his exceptionalism. Obituaries like these* demand that we sew the wings of angels on the Palestinian's back, so that he will then, and only then, become mournable.[6]

---

* "أن تنعى رجلاً فلسطينياً باللغة الإنكليزية يعني أن تعذب نفسك. تأمرنا هذه اللغة، المخطوطة على الصواريخ التي فتكت بك، أن نؤهلك للعزاء قبل العزاء، أن نبرّئك من خطاياك: جغرافيتك، ودينك، ولونك، وجنسك، وانتماءاتك؛ أن نستثنيك من صفوف مقاتلينا، ونقاتل لإظهار استثنائيتك، ونخيط أجنحة الملائكة والقديسين على ظهرك، فتصبح حينها، فقط حينها، قابلاً للرثاء بحكم مهنتك النبيلة، وتعليمك العالي، وقصائدك الخالية من الرصاص. نحن ببساطة لسنا موجودين في لغة المستعمر. إعلان وفاتك يستوجب انتشال الاعتراف بوجودك أصلاً، وانتشال الاعترافات هو جلد للذات أيضاً. تحول هذه اللغة جنازة الفلسطيني إلى ساحة حشد وإقناع وتثقيف، لا يوجد فيها مسلمات وحقائق موضوعية. في هذه المعادلة، لا يمكنني أن أعرّف العالم برفعت من دون أن أعرّفهم على حي الشجاعية، ولن يعرفوا الشجاعية من دون أن يعرفوا قطاع غزة، ولن يفهموا الأخير إن لم يفهموا فلسطين والاستعمار والصهيونية والنكبة. وهكذا، فترتدي عند النعي زي المؤرخ والناشط والمحلل السياسي، ونجعل من المواثيق والقوانين الدولية والإحصاءات مرجعية تتفشى في أسطر الرثاء، قد تنافس وتتفوق على إنجازاتك، وذكريات أحبائك، ومواقفك الطريفة، ورسائلنا إلى زوجتك وأطفالك."

TO MAKE SUCH ETHNOCENTRIC DEMANDS IS TO ABANDON THE PALESTINIANS who do not have the training and resources required to evade the category of the dehumanized. To abandon those of us who are bound to "err." "Respectability," like "congruence" and "moral authority," comes at a steep price, which, for most, is unobtainable. What about Palestinians who have not had the luxury to memorize the tropes one should avoid while agonizing? Those under the barrage of rockets or in solitary confinement? What is it to us if they can only obtain solace in expletives and hasty generalizations? What about Palestinians who simply do not wish to acquire an erudite lexicon? Those who refuse the rules of the game?

It is not controversial—or courageous—to say that, like the rest of the world, we are a complex nation with both "progressive" and "regressive" elements, however those categories are defined. Our dispositions, perceived or proven, should not grant our oppressors the opportunity to rewrite history or absolve themselves of guilt. This matters because most of the time, it is the poor and the underprivileged, the refugees and the besieged, who bear the brunt of Zionism.

Our believability as subjects of colonial violence is reliant on the ability to play the suffocating role of perfect victims, a role optimized by the upwardly mobile and institutionally backed among us, perhaps to protect that backing and mobility. But can your class ever escape you? Rejecting this script, refusing reverence, is unlikely to jeopardize the status of our elites, but it would, without a shadow of doubt, help raise the ceiling for Palestinians en masse.

THE POLITICS OF DEFANGING

Unfortunately, Palestinians who have made tonal and rhetorical "mistakes" (to say nothing of individuals who choose armed struggle) are often left to fight individual battles, in the academy, at the office, on the internet, fending for themselves against corporate retaliation, smear campaigns waged by powerful, plutocratic entities, and even finding themselves in jail.* I am not denying that politically conscious individuals of the Palestinian elite have historically opposed such entities fiercely (i.e., Canary Mission,† MEMRI,‡ and CAMERA§). Nor do I make the naive argument that our engagement in a politics of appeal is the reason the well of those entities has not dried. But the unwillingness to take discursive and affective risks, *calculated* risks, at the podium and in the public sphere reveals an unwillingness to disrupt the norms that sustain these organizations. Meanings, taboos, if not shattered, persist. Emperors, if not ridiculed, remain clothed.

Perhaps another way to examine this dilemma is by accepting that class blindness is not so much a bug or a feature of humanization but a main catalyst of the framework. If humanization can be understood as a "culture," or an aspira-

---

* See the stories of Samaher Esmail, Riddhi Patel, Bilal Al-Saadi, Ahmed Tobasi, Mustafa Sheta, and Jamal Abu Joas of the Freedom Theatre.

† A Zionist organization that operates as a blacklist, profiling students, educators, and professionals who are supportive of the Palestinian cause and the Boycott, Divestment, Sanctions (BDS) movement, often labeling them as bigots or "terror supporters" and hindering their career or academic prospects.

‡ A media watch group cofounded by a former Israeli military intelligence officer.

§ CAMERA was founded in 1982 to counter anti-Zionist and pro-Palestinian narratives in mainstream media.

48 PERFECT VICTIMS

tional social performance of sorts, then it is the invention of the gatekeepers of culture, who, invariably, are the elites. Ghassan Kanafani described patriarchy in Palestinian society as "the necessary result of a feudal mentality, of a political feudalism," as opposed to a spontaneous social condition.[7] He argued that it is a psychological phenomenon "insofar as class itself crystalizes psychological phenomena."[8] The same contention applies to the humanization project (even if it is regarded as a collective attitude, rather than a systemically sustained ideological practice). This becomes glaringly true when you consider how it has hindered the development of new and effective liberation strategies sensitive to current contexts. And when you consider how the project of humanization has negatively shaped public opinion regarding armed resistance and radical forms of political expression, not to mention progressive politics. And *especially* when you comprehend that our semantic "errors" are disciplined more emphatically than the colonizer's systemic violence. Humanization, then, is not merely our psychic response to colonial dehumanization—it exposes the absence of material analysis in our societies. As a project, it is largely the mandate of a specific class; "man . . . was one of the values invented by the bourgeoisie."[9] If not directly in service of class interests then certainly it is in service of classist worldviews, a world where the rich can master roles the poor cannot imagine auditioning for.

What promises to save you from dehumanization? Sophisticated degrees. The money in your bank account. The willingness to forgive. An unassuming gaze and unthreatening demeanor. Connections to the magazine editor who slanders your neighbors. At the bar, he asks his friend in the military to release you from the cell, as a favor, to go easy on you. You are worldly and politically correct. You are a prodigy—unlike the others. But what about the others? The others who suffocate under this shrinking definition of humanity? Those who were not privileged enough to go to a five-star university or be born into a line of feudal lords? What about those without halos, the angry men who wander the streets with mouths full of spit and venom, the children whose shoulders are burdened by the straps of rifles, the women who choose an explosive path? What about the poor? What about those who are cruel with the occupier and cruel with their kin? The not-so-gentle fathers? The reckless in our midst, those who would furrow the eyebrows of Europeans: the sister who "found her rage / in the kitchen drawer,"[10] and the sister "learning the anatomy of the gun"?[11] Do they not deserve life? According to whose law?

▼

* " ضِدُّ.. أن تدرسَ أختي عضلاتُ البندقيّة"

3. *shireen's passport*

On May 11, 2022, beloved Palestinian TV reporter and Al Jazeera veteran Shireen Abu Akleh was shot and killed by the Israeli occupation forces during a raid of the Jenin refugee camp in the occupied West Bank.

IF "THE PALESTINIAN" IS GUILTY BY BIRTH, then saving yourself from this original sin requires deserting—disowning—the Palestinian. Such a desertion is generally not your own doing; it is done on your behalf. You are banished from your Palestinianness, sometimes posthumously, through the kindness of political missionaries, rich in mercy, who "made you alive" even when you were "dead in your transgressions." You were once among the condemned, by nature deserving of wrath. But "by grace you have been saved."[1] They want to disarm your image in the minds of suspicious, spectating strangers, so they seize your rifles, the real and the imaginary. They raise you up and seat you in their realm. You lie still in an open casket, wearing other people's clothes.

WHEN I SAW HER LIFELESS BODY PLANTED FACE DOWN, next to an unnamed tree, on an unnamed street, I thought the world would stand still. A threshold had been crossed. A fixture of our televisions, a constant guest in our living rooms, the bearer of our news—good or bad, mostly bad—was now herself a news item. She had been murdered in cold blood, in broad daylight, her field execution broadcast in real time. I watched her murder on my phone on the way to the airport. Something told me the world would start anew. People everywhere would learn her name and what took her to Jenin, why the tree next to her had been riddled with bullets long before, and what the name of the street—Balat al-Shuhada—means. Within minutes of her assassination, I got a "tip" in my email inbox from a reporter: "Very urgent and necessary, please announce on Twitter and Facebook that Shireen Abu Aqleh* is an American citizen. This is a fact, not a rumor. The Israelis killed an American journalist." I did not "announce" that Shireen was a citizen of the United States. And when I wrote about her murder, I insisted to my editors that, if I must mention this fact, I would refer to her as a carrier of a US passport, not as an American citizen. Why contribute— even if only with a simple phrase—to a hierarchy of lives where citizenry, like race, class, gender, "civility," plays a role in determining whether someone deserves compassion or due diligence?

---

* Shireen Abu Akleh (1971–2022) was a Palestinian journalist from Jerusalem who spent twenty-five years as a television correspondent for Al Jazeera. On May 11, 2022, Shireen was targeted and killed by the Israeli occupation forces while covering an Israeli raid on the Jenin refugee camp.

SHIREEN'S PASSPORT

I wanted the world to stand still over the death of a Palestinian, regardless of qualifiers. But that didn't matter: within hours, the news spread like wildfire. Her passport was the talking point. Shireen was an American and her alleged Americanness swiftly made her human.

That email was undoubtedly well intentioned, but it felt like a slap in the face. The logic is straightforward: certain citizenships can transform the slain—usually a number in a given statistic—into a person of blood and flesh, a victim worthy of sympathy. The bald eagle embossed on Shireen's travel documents would make her even *more* worthy. Though not one to turn the other cheek, she certainly fit the obligatory profile of a perfect victim: a 51-year-old woman, a Christian, a journalist who was killed while wearing a clearly marked press vest and helmet, *and* a foreign national. Americans might die by the rifle of a "troubled" teenager in school hallways, but very rarely by the rifles of a foreign army. Palestinians, on the other hand, are shot every day with impunity. Barely three weeks after Shireen's assassination, Ghofran Warasneh,* a reporter from Hebron's Al-Arroub refugee camp, was killed by the Israeli occupation forces as she was on her way to work.[2] Despite being a journalist, her killing barely made a splash in the Arab world, let alone in the West.

Like all those who reiterated the line "Shireen Abu Akleh is American," the reporter who sent the email had to have

---

* Ghofran Warasneh (1991–2022) was a Palestinian journalist from Hebron. In January 2022, six months before the Israeli military killed her, she was sentenced to three months of imprisonment.

54 PERFECT VICTIMS

believed it could lead to some form of accountability. The US is idle when its biggest ally slaughters the stateless, but when a citizen is the victim of *that* kind of violence, there *must* be consequences. Violence—suddenly, surprisingly—becomes deplorable. Killing journalists becomes more scandalous and easier to denounce when they are Americans or Europeans. Citizenship, in this worldview, flings Shireen away from the crime of being Palestinian and closer to blamelessness, increasing her chances of recourse. It is "strategic," some might argue. But then Rachel Corrie comes to mind.[*]

And so does Omar As'ad.[†] Neither citizenship nor old age could save him from the Israeli soldiers who would gag, bind, and blindfold him, leaving him to die on the cold ground. And the injured young man at the Rafah crossing, Yusef Sha'ban, who held his open US passport next to his bruised face and pleaded with a mouth full of blood, "Where is the country whose citizenship I hold? Why will it not protect me?"[‡]

Still, there is no denying that there *is* a hierarchy of lives, that passports *are* a currency. They help world leaders appraise your

---

[*] Rachel Corrie (1979–2003) was a 23-year-old peace activist from Olympia, Washington, and a member of the International Solidarity Movement. On March 16, 2003, she was crushed to death by an Israeli bulldozer while protesting the destruction of a Palestinian home in the Gaza Strip.

[†] Omar As'ad was an eighty-year-old Palestinian man who was killed during an Israeli raid in the village of Jiljilya on the outskirts of Ramallah in the occupied West Bank. As'ad was stopped at 2:30 a.m. and forced out of his car, blindfolded, handcuffed, and dragged to a construction site. Left there by the IOF, he died of a heart attack. See Al Tahhan, "Elderly Palestinian Man."

[‡] "أمريكي في غزة يناشد واشنطن إخلاءه مع أسرته" الأناضول، ٢٠/تشرين الأول/٢٠٢٣.

SHIREEN'S PASSPORT

tragedy, and their reactions rely on this appraisal—transforming a quotidian elimination of a Palestinian into a dreadful killing of an American journalist, a despicable attack on press freedom, a travesty. Passports as a currency help people buy your story. Citizens—of *certain* countries, of course—command a larger audience and a louder uproar when they are targeted by Israeli violence. But what did Rachel Corrie's Americanness give her outside of that uproar? Did it deliver justice for her family? Did it stop the bulldozer that crushed her from demolishing more homes? Do Americans murdered by Israeli settlers receive the same kind of state-sponsored grief as the Americans held hostage in Gaza? What did the hyphen in Omar Asʿad's nationality offer him beyond a spot in the headlines that otherwise ignore the unhyphenated? Did those headlines name the culprit, or was Asʿad just "found dead"?

My argument is not that we should stop using political and diplomatic maneuvers to coerce powerful regimes into action or in hopes of changing their anticipated stances. I am arguing that we reassess such tactics, taking into consideration their long- and short-term side effects, and ask whether they are worth the gamble. When a passport becomes a political device for "humanization," the pretext is to coax Western governments to "seek justice" on behalf of their citizens. But the subtext, more dangerously, more humiliatingly, is selling a narrative of innocence, a narrative that accepts the racist and xenophobic worldviews of the audience it attempts to persuade.

PERFECT VICTIMS

ONE COULD ARGUE THAT THE ENDS JUSTIFY THE MEANS. But what are those "ends"? Justice? Truth? When Shireen was targeted, did Western media outlets name the sniper? The Associated Press altered and then redacted a quote by the Palestinian Ministry of Health so that it no longer named Israeli forces as the culprit; the headline from the *New York Times* read exactly as you would expect: "A Trailblazing Palestinian Journalist Dies, Aged 51."[3] In another article, the paper deceived its readers by claiming that Al Jazeera said she died amid "clashes between the Israeli military and Palestinian gunmen," despite Al Jazeera's direct reports that Israeli gunfire killed Shireen. The eyewitness reports of journalists on the scene—one of whom was also shot by Israeli gunfire—were rarely cited.

When occupation forces attacked Abu Akleh's funeral in Jerusalem two days later, how did mainstream newscasters narrate it?* Did they report the IOF storming Saint Joseph Hospital, where the funeral began, to assault mourners, patients, and staff alike?[4] Or when they smashed the back window of the hearse, stole the Palestinian flag covering her coffin, and attacked the pallbearers so rabidly that it almost fell to the ground? What did correspondents call it? "Tussling" and "clashes."[5] Shireen wasn't

---

* The IOF had demanded that only a small number of mourners—and only Christians, at that—attend the funeral and that anticolonial chants be banned, likely fearing that parading Palestinian national symbols around Jerusalem would threaten the Israeli regime's perceived "sovereignty" over the occupied city. It was another episode of the ongoing war on anticolonial expression, be it political anger or communal grief. Abu Akleh's family rejected the restrictions, and so the beatings began.

SHIREEN'S PASSPORT

the first Palestinian to be persecuted in death: a 1976 *Al-Ittihad* newspaper headline reads, "Three New Flowers in the Bouquet of Martyrs: Mass Arrests and Assaults on Funerals." Nor will she be the last.

Three days after her burial, Israeli soldiers brutally beat those carrying 23-year-old Walid Sharif's casket inside the cemetery where he was laid to rest.[6] The IOF had injured Walid inside Al-Aqsa Mosque compound on the third Friday of Ramadan, and he later succumbed to his wounds.[7] Despite the ridiculous restrictions and extremely late burial time imposed by the Occupation authorities, thousands of Palestinians attended his funeral. Fifty-two of them were injured, and thirty-seven were hospitalized. One of the martyr's relatives, Nader Sharif, was hit by a rubber-coated bullet, which caused him to lose his eye and suffer severe skull injuries.* When the confrontations faded, Palestinians were left to clean the tear gas canisters and stun grenades from their beloveds' tombstones. Two weeks after that, Ghofran Warasneh's funeral was attacked. The military intercepted the ambulance transporting her body into Al-Arroub refugee camp, where she would be buried, which forced the mourners to carry her corpse on their shoulders. In spite of soldiers' brutality, the burial ceremony was finalized in the camp.†

---

* Nader was arrested the following day from a Jerusalem hospital, and his family members at his bedside were assaulted in the process. See "۲۰۲۲/أيار/۱۷ اعتدت على عائلته.. الاحتلال يعتقل المصاب نادر الشريف" شبكة قدس الإخبارية.

† "۲۰۲۲/حزيران/۷.اغتالها الاحتلال الإسرائيلي واعترض جثمانها.. الفلسطينيون يشيعون الصحفية والأسيرة المحررة غفران وراسنة" الجزيرة

58 PERFECT VICTIMS

Although routine and relentless, these acts of desecration do not often receive international media attention.

When it comes to Palestine, the sacred laws of journalism are bendable. Optional even. Passive voice is king. Omitting facts is standard. Fabrication is permissible. Journalists become stenographers, and reporters become state secretaries, as they parrot police and military narratives. They tamper with evidence. They muddle, mislead, and misconstrue, manufacturing consent for ethnic cleansing and creating confusion around murders that are clear as day. The courageous industry that boasts of speaking "truth to power" is but a bullhorn for the powerful. We have seen this time and time again. It is almost satirical: anchors reject the data before their eyes to recite lies, and newspapers read like caricatures of themselves. When a 2014 Israeli airstrike on a cafe in Gaza blew eight Palestinians to shreds,[8] the headline from the *New York Times* was "Missile at Beachside Gaza Cafe Finds Patrons Poised for World Cup."* Whose missile? Whose gunfire? Who is the sniper?

---

* Notably, the *Times* did not name any of the Palestinians killed by the Israeli naval fire. An hour after publication the headline was changed to "Missile Kills 8 at Beachside Gaza Cafe," then, a couple of hours later, it was changed again for a final time, this time not only obfuscating the culprit, but removing the missile altogether. See Akram, "In Rubble of Gaza."

SHIREEN'S PASSPORT 59

IN THE CASE OF GHOFRAN WARASNEH, whom Israeli soldiers shot at the checkpoint barricading her occupied hometown, it was not merely the lack of a passport—statelessness—that made her an uncompelling victim. It was the soldiers' justification for murdering her that classified her death a mundane elimination of a Palestinian. The army advertised the usual narrative: she was intending to commit a stabbing attack, armed with a knife that was nowhere to be found.[9] Even though unfounded, this narrative revoked her "civility," placing her alongside those whose killing is not only legal but nonnegotiable: Palestinian militants. And so Ghofran became a feeble subject to the same human rights and press freedom organizations that rushed to Shireen Abu Akleh's defense.* After all, who would want to defend an alleged assailant?†

The question is rhetorical, but it should not be. We and our allies have spent generations reiterating the Palestinian People's right of resistance, be it through situating our struggle for liberation in a global context (*The US considered Nelson Mandela a terrorist until 2008*), or citing international law (*United Nations General Assembly Resolution 37/43 reaffirms . . . ;‡ According to*

---

* By "defense" I mean pathetically calling for "an independent investigation."
† Perhaps exploiting the hierarchy of lives as a humanization tactic only proves useful when it comes to "neutral civilians" who, unlike Rachel Corrie, will not stand in the face of a bulldozer to oppose ethnic cleansing. But even so-called neutrality has not historically been able to save or protect the Palestinian.
‡ G.A. Res. 37/43, "Importance of the universal realization of the right of peoples to self-determination and of the speedy granting of independence to colonial countries and peoples for the effective guarantee and observance of human rights," December 3, 1982.

Protocol I of the Geneva Conventions . . .), or quoting revolutionary thinkers (*The work of the colonized is to imagine every possible method for annihilating the colonist*).[10] Yet when decolonization abandons the conceptual to chase after its material manifestations, many of us tend to lose our compass.

In other words, when a Palestinian individual tangibly engages in armed struggle, their struggle, even on a discursive level, remains individual. Many of us bury our heads in the sand, pretending not to see the Palestinians with the knives, rifles, or Molotov cocktails. We do not editorialize freedom fighters' stories the way we do the stories of the brutalized. We do not rally behind them the way we rally behind the unarmed and those "executed extrajudicially," which inadvertently reinforces the colonizer's self-appointed jurisdiction atop our stolen land. We waste our time fixating on whether the knife was planted next to the slain—*which it often is*—instead of fixating on why the slain might have sought to pick up a knife in the first place. But if the "society that drives its members to desperate solutions is . . . a society that needs to be replaced,"[11] and if we have the moral and legal right to violent resistance against colonial powers, why *not* defend an alleged assailant?

SHIREEN'S PASSPORT

THE INVENTION OF THE CIVILIAN as a "nonpartisan," "neutral" figure has exacerbated the depoliticization of the Palestinian cause. To be deemed a civilian necessitates that we exist in a mythological dimension where we are without perspective. Our cause, as imagined in this mythology, is no longer understood as a liberation struggle but as a "humanitarian crisis," where revolutionaries are not part and parcel of our nation, motivated by political aspirations and dreams of emancipation. Instead, they are interpreted as rogue actors senselessly wreaking havoc to the dismay of helpless bystanders—the disinterested women and children, the impartial paramedics and journalists.

In such ahistorical readings, which obfuscate the power imbalance between the occupier and the occupied, the militant is evacuated outside of the context that gave rise to him or her in the first place; the newscaster is expected to present the killing of her siblings as if she were an unbiased observer; and the nurse whose patient is a beloved coworker maimed by an airstrike is expected to maintain "professionalism," to not seek revenge on the drone operator. In this dimension, the *fida'i* reemerges as "a figure that closely resembles the Zionist soldier, capable of committing 'war crimes' against 'civilians' in the heart of 'Tel Aviv.'"[12] This, as Orouba Othman writes, "obscures the fact that the armed militant is a victim who first inherits from his ancestors the conditions of dispossession, expulsion and mutilation, and later transforms these abstractions into the motive force of decolonization."[13]

The militant, whether in Gaza or Jenin, is not an inexplicable phenomenon or a "freak of nature." Nor is he just a descendant of Nakba survivors who were forced from their homes in Jaffa and Al-Naqab, carrying their bitter anger decades after it has gone stale. The militant confronts his own Nakbas every day, his fury is resuscitated each time he is strip-searched on the streets of Jerusalem or beaten with rifle butts at the Qalandiya military checkpoint. Each displacement, each demolition, each premature funeral adds fuel to his fire. Each sibling he buries or visits in prison, each bullet that ambushes his colleagues, each rocket polluting his sky reignites him.

My instinct, writing in English, is to offer context explaining why a group of young men would want to take up arms against their occupiers,[14] to ask the audience the basic question posed by Rashid Hussein:* "After they have burned my homeland, my friends, and my youth, / how can my poems not turn into guns?"[15]† But the Global North has shown, especially in recent years, that it doesn't need context to justify resistance to occupations. Resistance, in the Western mind, is not defined by the act itself, that is, defending oneself or one's community against an oppressive force. Rather, resistance is defined on the basis of its perpetrators.

In 2022, I tried to help my friend Ru'a Rimawi publish an opinion essay about her late brothers, Jawad and Thafer Rimawi, two young Palestinian men shot by the occupation forces during

---

* Born in Haifa, Palestine, Rashid Hussein (1936–1977) was a poet, teacher, orator, and a founding member of the 1959 Land Movement. He died in a "mysterious" apartment fire in New York City.

† "بعد إحراق بلادي ورفاقي وترابي
كيفَ لا تصبحُ أشعاري!" بنادقُ!"

a raid of their village, where the IOF has no business being. They were killed within minutes of each other.[16] We pitched the story to the *Guardian*, the *Washington Post*, and the *Los Angeles Times* (we didn't try the *New York Times*). All publications refused or ignored the article. When we talked to a media expert about this, his opinion was that Ru'a's article was not getting published because her brothers threw stones at the Israeli army, because they spent their last moments honorably defending their community against colonial violence. Resistance, in their case, meant something profane, disgraceful, not suitable for readers. Their victimhood was not a perfect victimhood, so they were not offered a spot in the *LA Times*.[17]

Yet in the same month that Ru'a was trying to publish her brothers' story, the *LA Times* ran a headline that read "Kyiv Civilians Take Up Arms . . . to Fight Russian Attack on Ukraine."[18] *Civilians*. The *Washington Post* printed a similar headline.[19] The *Guardian* profiled "Ukraine's Student Molotov Cocktail-Makers."[20] The *New York Post* published an article with a headline praising a "heroic" Ukrainian suicide bomber.[21] *In the same month* that Ru'a was turned away from one publication after the other because her brothers dared resist the occupation, Sky News broadcast what can essentially be described as a Molotov-making workshop: "Civilians Help Make Molotov Cocktails to Take On Russian Forces."[22] The *New York Times* interviewed a psychologist who advised that "anger and hate" in the context of occupation "is a normal reaction and important to validate," stating that such hate should be "channel[ed] into something useful," like "making incendiary bombs."[23]

64 PERFECT VICTIMS

ON THE PAGES OF THE *NEW YORK TIMES*, as "[Ukrainian] insurgent activity is now intensifying,"[24] "[Hamas fighters] hide under residential neighborhoods."[25] "The [Ukrainian] fighters strike stealthily in environs they know intimately, using car bombs, booby traps and targeted killings with pistols,"[26] while Hamas fighters are "storing their weapons in miles of tunnels and in houses, mosques, sofas."[27] On the pages of the *Times*, both people are "blending into the local population,"[28] "blurring the boundary between civilians and combatants."[29] The paper says, "these practices mean that Hamas is responsible for many of the civilian deaths, according to international law."[30] But it gloats that the Amnesty International report accusing the Ukrainian military of violating international laws and risking civilian lives by operating in hospitals, residential neighborhoods, and schools[31] "was met with widespread and almost universal condemnation."[32]

---

* A comprehensive *New York War Crimes* study ("Words Like Slaughter") comparing the *Times* coverage of the genocidal war on Gaza to its coverage of the invasion of Ukraine, found that the paper legitimized and glorified the Ukrainian military and underground resistance groups "unequivocally," all the while condemning Palestinian resisters, "who are generally cast as terrorists and rarely have their motivations, perspective or strategies explained." The *New York War Crimes* is a free newspaper distributed by Writers Against the War on Gaza (WAWOG). Since its first issue on November 9, 2023—which listed the names of 2,608 martyrs killed by the IOF—the paper has published twelve themed issues, including "Media Manufactures Consent for Genocide" and "Revolution and Resistance until Liberation and Return." "Weaponizing the widespread visual recognition of the *Times* as a voice of authority," the paper is influenced by ACT UP's paper the *New York Crimes*, which began circulation in 1988, near the beginning of the US AIDS epidemic. Isack, "Stealing the Voice of Authority."

SHIREEN'S PASSPORT   65

Your conclusion as a reader of the *Times* is as follows: Ukrainians go to war in the concrete jungle because they, unlike Palestinians, "have fewer and fewer options when it comes to where they locate their forces." Ukraine is "defending itself against a Russian army that has vastly more firepower."[33] But "Hamas's tactics [in the most densely populated place on earth] explain why Israel has been forced to strike so much civilian infrastructure, kill so many Palestinians and detain so many civilians."[34]

Resistance, in the Western mind, is a mutating concept. While Ukrainian resistance is glorified for its guerrilla warfare tactics, Palestinian resistance—termed "terrorism"—is puzzling, perverted, and pathological. Mainstream media's insistence on these framings is not due to any fundamental differences in the ways both peoples exercise violence. Nor is it solely because of Ukrainians' skin color; one needs to look no further than the Irish Republican Army to see that whiteness alone is no golden ticket—at least not in a war against British colonialism.

Rather, the tonal shift employed in media coverage is simply in service of the West's strategic interests. While the Israeli settler-colonial regime is the United States' most important ally in the Middle East, and practically an offshoot of Europe, created to protect Western imperialism, Russia represents an "existential" threat to the West.[35] Thus, it is not so much of a surprise that newspapers owned and operated by the ruling classes delegitimize Palestinian rebellion in the same pages where they celebrate that of Ukrainians. To sustain the Zionist project in Palestine, to protect the empire's capitalistic and militaristic endeavors in the region, the Palestinian freedom fighter must fall. And so the empire's stenographers standardize the dehumanization of Palestinians and the demonization of their resistance. How many Palestinians were murdered by the very forces and institutions that demand they remain "neutral" and "nonpartisan" if they want to maintain their "innocence"? We are all, in some way or another, terrorists in the eyes of the paper of record.

AND WHO AMONG THE "TERRORISTS" IS INNOCENT?
In a CNN interview, Christiane Amanpour, who made a name for herself covering the Bosnian genocide, probes a prominent Israeli author: "Can I ask you, because you are a *really thoughtful person* . . . Is there a moral maze? Is there an ability to hold two thoughts at one time?" The author shakes his head in either disbelief or amusement, then he interrupts her question with a scoff. Amanpour continues, "That that slaughter [on October 7] is the worst thing that could have happened, and that everybody has the right to live with rights and dignity, including the Palestinian people?" She quickly clarifies, perhaps correcting herself: "And I am *not* talking about Hamas."[36]

Through her resounding exclusion of Hamas from the category of those entitled "to live with rights and dignity," Amanpour effectively suggests that the supposedly universal Declaration of Human Rights can be conditioned upon one's political affiliations. Similar suggestions would spark outrage if uttered in relation to *any* other contemporary political party or any group. This, of course, is only an interpretation. But why dissect Amanpour's remarks when there are countless examples of annihilatory rhetoric that do not require reading between the lines? Why not focus on the sitting politicians describing Palestinians as "savages" that "have to be eradicated";[37] politicians whose battle cries are "finish them,"[38] "level the place,"[39] and "bounce the rubble in Gaza";[40] politicians who, when asked about our children, say with enthusiasm, "We should kill 'em all"?[41]

Wouldn't the explicitness of these comments make them easier to denounce, or at least easier to report? Shouldn't

68   PERFECT VICTIMS

unambiguity prevent misinterpretation? If so, why did the *New York Times* omit that the Israeli defense minister referred to Palestinians as "human animals" when it reported his instructions to tighten the siege on Gaza by cutting off water, electricity, and food? When the Israeli president addressed the international press, bellowing that "an entire nation is responsible," why did the *Financial Times* hastily remove his quote, "It is not true this rhetoric about civilians not being aware, not involved" from its broadsheet?*

Considering that the most brazen declarations are obfuscated from even nut grafs and margins, why bring up the subtle? Because in that subtlety one finds a more dangerous, more insidious logic. Examining the conversation between a liberal television anchor and a liberal author unveils the implicit underpinnings of their discourse: Palestinians must denounce certain affiliations, determined by the West, to be considered worthy of living. Or, I should correct myself, worthy of *condolences*, as we are doomed regardless. Bombs do not discriminate on the basis of political ideology: they take the liberal and the radical, the Salafist and the secular, the communist and the capitalist, sometimes from under the same roof. When the sniper finds your bedroom in the scope of his rifle, he (or she)† does not

---

* The quotation, originally published in the ninth graf, was deleted within the same day, though no editor's note was included, as is customary to notify readers of the significant change made to a piece after its initial release. Kerr et al., "Israel Calls for Evacuation."

† Feminism!

care whether the photograph beside your bed is of Nasrallah, Gandhi, or Haifa Wehbe. The photograph is only useful when your character is on trial.

This is the tension in which we exist: in response to "the bad guys" saying that there are no innocents among us, "the good guys" will retort that indeed there are innocents *if you look hard enough*. You hear it everywhere, in White House press briefings, in the halls of the European Union, even in the paragraphs of an ally's impassioned op-ed: *Not all Palestinians are Hamas*. And it is true that not all Palestinians support Hamas. But what is the implication of that argument? By distinguishing Palestinians from Hamas (or differentiating the supporters of the organization from its opponents, the members from the nonmembers), Amanpour, if I were to give her the benefit of the doubt, wanted to convince her Israeli guest of Palestinian humanity. But in her attempt to do so, it could be inferred that she implicitly condemned Hamas members and supporters to die. For when she insisted that she is "not talking about Hamas," she pledged allegiance to the belief that underpins both Israeli and American societies, across the political spectrum: unless Palestinians perform a preapproved sociopolitical disposition, one remains without an obligation to even pretend they are human.

One week after his interview with Amanpour, the *"really thoughtful"* liberal author went on a Japanese TV channel and asserted that the settler state "could defend itself with all the weapons it has, including nuclear capabilities."[42]

OF COURSE, IN PALESTINE, LIKE EVERYWHERE ELSE, there are individuals who are or define themselves as "apolitical." There are, one could argue, medics who think all parties are to blame, journalists who believe in the myth of objectivity instead of satirizing it. But "neutrality" is not an indicator of innocence, nor does it guarantee safety. In fact, what unites the nonpartisan and the partisan, or the partisan by association, is their susceptibility to settler violence. The difference is, we seem to only run to the rescue of those perceived to be apolitical. When the affiliated (or the allegedly affiliated) are a target, we first try to negate their alleged affiliation before we respond to their calls.

Some months into the ongoing genocide in Gaza, which is "the deadliest conflict for journalists in recent history," the Israeli occupation forces openly considered journalists employed by media organizations associated with or run by Hamas "to be legitimate military targets." A senior spokesperson for the IOF went as far as telling reporters that "there was 'no difference' between working for [Al-Aqsa TV] and belonging to Hamas's armed wing."[43] This statement brings to mind another comment by a different military spokesman, who said the late Shireen Abu Akleh was "armed with [her] camera."[44] It also brings to mind a *Jewish Insider* headline that reads, "One-Third of Journalists Killed in Gaza Were Affiliated with Terrorist Groups."[45] A headline where journalists justify killing journalists.

The instinct of many defenders of Palestinians is to dispel the connection between the slain Palestinian media workers and their supposed political leanings, as if anywhere in the

SHIREEN'S PASSPORT

world these exist in isolation. While it is demanded of us to distance ourselves from the guerrilla fighters struggling against colonialism and occupation, Zionist soldiers—the colonizers and occupiers—can work, without much irony or scrutiny, in newsrooms and in media watchdog organizations. Take, for example, *Axios*'s political reporter covering Israeli affairs, Barak Ravid, who was, until March 2023, a reservist in the Israeli occupation forces while working for an international media outlet. Or the editor-in-chief of the *Atlantic*, Jeffrey Goldberg, who dropped out of his American university to volunteer in the IOF during the First Intifada, then, during the course of his job as a so-called prison counsellor at the notorious Ketziot camp, lied to cover up for a friend whom he witnessed beating a prisoner.[46] Correspondents entangled with the Israeli army are not challenged on the basis of proximity to "the conflict," let alone condemned to die because of their participation in or fondness of the Israeli military apparatus.[47] They do not need to be humanized.

Indeed, they are often more than merely human; the *New Yorker* had no reservations in quoting what it called a "lefty" journalist who lauded the IOF soldiers *waging* the genocide in Gaza with the words "they are our children. . . . They are us."[48] If you are a *New York Times* correspondent in occupied Jerusalem, as Isabel Kershner was, with two sons in the IOF, how does that influence your reporting on "the conflict"?[49] If your spouse's professional duty was "shaping a positive image of Israel in the media,"[50] as program director at the Institute for National Security Studies (INSS), the settler state's "leading

72　　　　　　　　　　PERFECT VICTIMS

security think tank,"[51] as was Kershner's husband's,* how can you maintain impartiality as a reporter? "An examination of articles that Kershner has written or contributed to since 2009 reveals that she overwhelmingly relies on the INSS for think tank analysis about events in the region."[52] Examples of reporters having direct ties to the entity waging the genocide against the Palestinian People are numerous.† As for Palestinians—we are held to a completely different and impossible standard.

It is not enough for a Palestinian to be a journalist to be deemed human; they must be "unaffiliated." Otherwise, in accordance with Zionist logic, they cannot be grievable or included in the official death toll; slaughtering them is cause for celebration. Such an unfeasible demand of "no affiliation" fragments Palestinians further: we are not only divided based on colonial borders and invented geographies, but even within a single profession we are split into legitimate and illegitimate targets. This has created a reality in which the Palestinian People are pitted against each other; some of us work for reputable, foreign agencies, others work for local ones, "Hamas-run." As

---

* His name is Hirsh Goodman.
† Former *New York Times* Jerusalem bureau chief Joel Greenberg served in the IOF. The son of another former *Times* Jerusalem bureau chief and the senior editor of the Middle East at *Bloomberg News*, Ethan Bronner, has a son who served in the IOF. David Brooks, a conservative columnist at the *Times*, also has a son who served in the IOF, as does Andrew Revkin, who was the *Times*'s *Dot Earth* blogger. See *Electronic Intifada*, "*New York Times* Fails"; Weir, "US Media and Israeli Military"; Weisberg, "David Brooks"; Revkin, "My Stroke of Luck."

a result of this indictment, we look for the exceptional, and we cite it.

And when I say "we," I implicate myself in this critique. When writing Omar As'ad's story in the previous pages, I wasted some time searching for reliable sources that proved the soldiers had beaten him. Something, perhaps a deeply seated, learned behavior or a pervasive, subconscious impulse, told me it was not enough that he had been left to die in the cold—bound, gagged, and blindfolded. He needed to have been beaten too. Despite the entire argument I am agonizing over in this book, I sifted through articles in an attempt to editorialize his killing with another layer of brutality. But when we do what we do to Shireen Abu Akleh, to Omar As'ad, to Hind Rajab, to Mohammed Abu Khdeir, when we do it out of love, out of a desperate desire to legitimize mourning them, we are inadvertently reifying the colonial rationale that killed them and rendered them killable in the first place.

THOSE OF US WHO DID NOT FLAG SHIREEN'S PASS-PORT, waving it like an exonerating piece of evidence at a defamation trial, did something else. We cited, over and over, her bloodied vest and helmet in an effort to exculpate her from the crime of being Palestinian. On the day she was murdered, Israeli forces killed eighteen-year-old Thaer Yazouri in Al-Bireh City near Ramallah* and used sixteen-year-old Ahed Mereb as a human shield in Jenin.[53] On that same day, they also shot 23-year-old Rami Srour after falsely accusing him of attempting to stab a soldier in Jerusalem's Old City.† Neither of the three wore a press vest, so they stayed confined to the expendables' domain.

But Shireen Abu Akleh—even in a press vest and a helmet—was not a neutral bystander. "Armed with her camera," she dedicated decades of her life to uncovering the truth. She was one of us, through and through. She rejoiced when we rejoiced and mourned when we mourned. So why distance her from the rest of her people? Why divorce her from Fatima, Leila, Rasmea, Khalida, Dalal, and the many women who used various means to resist the occupation? In Jenin, one woman marching behind Shireen's casket testified to filming journalists, "[Shireen] was in the rubble looking for martyrs . . . in Jenin camp during the [2002 Israeli] invasion. . . . She helped me look for my children."[54]

In a Facebook post from July 2021, Shireen wrote an almost prophetic sentence: "Some absence brings forth a greater presence."

---

* "٢٠٢٣/أيار/١١ تشييع جثمان الشهيد الفتى ثائر اليازوري" وكالة معًا .

† "٢٠٢٣/أيار/١٧ قرار بالإفراج عن الطفل المصاب رامي سرور" بوابة الهدف الإخبارية .

SHIREEN'S PASSPORT

Indeed, her absence united the Palestinian People across class, religion, gender, and political affiliation. Palestinians gave her what one of her colleagues called the "longest funeral in recent Palestinian history . . . 40 [kilometers] of love."* Her Jerusalem procession was, in fact, the fourth one organized to mourn her death; the others took place in Nablus, Ramallah, and Jenin, where Israeli snipers killed her.

In Jerusalem, hundreds of thousands participated in the funeral. Holders of green ID cards jumped over the Wall and snuck into the city from the West Bank. Busloads came from within 1948-occupied Palestine. Strangers offered each other embraces and condolences. They marched from Saint Joseph Hospital to the Catholic church and through Jaffa Gate to the cemetery where she was finally laid to rest. Dozens of Palestinian flags flew all around the occupied holy city. It was a scene like no other. And despite the bruises and batons, the land spoke Arabic.†

The chanting crowds forced the start of a new chapter of the battle over our city, which for decades saw rapid colonial expansion and shrinking of the Palestinian presence.‡ Albeit temporar-

---

* Rania Zabane at Al Jazeera.

† The reference is to the wildly famous 1960s song "El ard btitkallim 'araby" (الأرض بتتكلم عربي), by the Egyptian singer-composer Sayyed Makkawi. The lyrics were written by the Egyptian poet Fouad Haddad.

‡ This kind of gathering has been off-limits to Palestinians in recent years. Since three Israelis kidnapped, killed, and burned sixteen-year-old Mohammed Abu Khdeir in 2014, Jerusalem began to resemble itself less and less. Because of heavy scrutiny and persecution by Israeli police and Musta'ribeen

ily, her funeral catapulted us into a glorious, emancipated future. Everyone was there: the stay-at-homes, the engineers, the stone throwers, the self-described apolitical passersby, the paramedics, the students, the elderly bus drivers, the clergy. For a fleeting moment, the wounds didn't hurt, the jail-time didn't matter, the tear gas wasn't so bad. For a fleeting moment, Shireen Abu Akleh liberated Jerusalem, and Jerusalem, in turn, gave her a funeral fit for a martyr.

▼

(Israeli military and police undercover intelligence units famous for dressing and speaking like Palestinians and blending into crowds as agents provocateurs and carrying out arrests and beatings), Palestinians' political or social gatherings have become nearly nonexistent. During the 2021 Unity Uprising, bare-chested youth confronted heavily armed soldiers for their right to sit, eat, sing, and protest at Damascus Gate—once the beating heart of Jerusalem, now plagued with surveillance cameras, military watchtowers, and police ready to brutalize people. During Ramadan that same year, Palestinians fought to preserve the status of Al-Aqsa Mosque compound, not only one of Islam's holiest sites but also a hub for social, political, and educational Palestinian activities. Shireen Abu Akleh's funeral—at the Jaffa Gate—marks a reclamation of public space.

4. *a life in cross-examination*

> *and I made up my mind that I was not one bit*
> *better than the meanest on earth . . .*
> —Eugene V. Debs[1]

CHIMPANZEE SOCIETIES WAGE WAR AGAINST EACH OTHER. Crows make and use tools. Dolphins talk to each other and talk about us. They have different dialects and various synonyms for "human" (some of them are slurs). Language, as such, is not what distinguishes us from other creatures that roam the earth. Nor is it intelligence. Sentiments—complex, sophisticated sentiment—it is said, are what make humans unique. How we refine or distort our emotions, codify them into structures, how we systematize our layered and recursive interior lives, how we immortalize our fleeting expressions into art, policy, or poison is what makes us stand out. Or so we tell ourselves.

In the framework of humanization, Palestinians are not entirely deprived of "uniquely human emotions," however, the Palestinian's affective allowance—the range of sentiments one is permitted to express openly—is extremely restricted and shrinks with every perceived "wrongdoing." We are allowed to

78 PERFECT VICTIMS

be hospitable (Yosef Weitz, the "Architect of Transfer,"* wrote in his diary about the unsuspecting Palestinians who served him food and welcomed him in homes he later stole).† We are implored to be peaceful (or submissive) and forbearing, and we are tolerated when we are. We are meek and we shall inherit no earth. What we are not allowed is the future: we cannot be ambitious or cunning; we cannot aspire to sovereignty or revenge. We are robbed of the right to complexity, to contradictory feelings, the right to "contain multitudes."‡ Our sadness is without teeth. Perhaps we can be bitter (see: "Palestinian Rejectionism"), but belligerence and hostility—foreign concepts to our oppressors, apparently—exile us outside of humanity once more. The only thing we are permitted to look forward to is the day's end.

---

* Yosef Weitz (1890–1972) was a Polish Jew who settled in Palestine in 1908 and later became the director of the Land and Afforestation Department at the Jewish National Fund (JNF). He sat in the first and second Transfer Committees, designed to deal with "the Arab problem." Known as the "Architect of Transfer"—with "transfer" being a euphemism for ethnic cleansing—Weitz played a key role in the forced expulsion of the Indigenous Palestinian population during the Nakba. He is also affectionately called the "Father of the Forests" by Israelis for his work at the JNF: cultivating forests on top of the ruins of depopulated Palestinian villages to conceal them.

† ‏יו חִסוי. סינבל יתוררגאו ינמוי.‏

‡ Walt Whitman or something.

A LIFE IN CROSS-EXAMINATION 79

**IN HIS CANONICAL AND BREATHTAKINGLY BEAUTI-
FUL 1973 POEM** "Abd el-Hadi Fights a Superpower," Taha
Muhammad Ali tells a jury that his illiterate "client," Abd
el-Hadi, has never toppled a tree or slain a cow or "spoken of the
New York Times behind its back," only ever raising his voice to
show hospitality—"Come in / by God, you will come in."† If he
were to encounter "the entire crew / of the aircraft carrier *Enterprise*,"‡ he would insist on providing the Navy Seals breakfast.
"Eggs / sunny-side up, / and labneh / fresh from the bag."² I know
many Abd el-Hadis: agreeable and amicable men whose generos-
ity precedes them. My beloved father is the first to come to mind,
only he preferred boiled eggs and hummus.

What a burden it is to live in a world that expects us to be
a nation of Abd el-Hadis. I shared this frustration with some
friends, mostly media workers, at a pub in London the day the

---

* Palestinian poet and short story writer. He was born in 1931 in Saffuriyya,
Galilee, before it was depopulated and destroyed by Zionist forces. He was
then expelled to Lebanon in 1948 and died in Nazareth, occupied Palestine, in 2011.

† Notably, the poem's official translation introduces a "please" before "come
in," perhaps to elucidate the warmth of the original word تفضل (*tfaddal*), or
perhaps it is an effort to make Abd el-Hadi more docile and agreeable than
he already is. In other contexts, tfaddal could mean an aggressive "Here!
Take it!" or a sarcastic way of saying "would you look at that." The literal
meaning is "to bestow" or "to deign," as in, "grace us with your presence,"
with the different registers of politeness or sarcasm that could suggest.

‡ US Navy aircraft carrier ship, the longest ever built and the first to be out-
fitted with nuclear weapons. It was deployed in most US imperial wars since
WWII, from the Cuban Missile Crisis and the Vietnam War, to Iraq and
Afghanistan.

Metropolitan police were looking for me.* My sentiment did not come from out of the blue. Our mutual friend Ahmed Alnaouq,† who lost twenty-one members of his family in Gaza at the hands of Zionists, had shared on social media that he does not hate the Jewish people.‡ The world I am complaining about operates under the same rules as the nonessential clause tucked within the last line: words enclosed between commas communicate superfluous information. If those nonessential words are removed, the sentence remains coherent and grammatically correct. In this case, Ahmed's twenty-one relatives buried under rubble become a mere subclause of the main point: he declared that he does not hate Jews. Meaning, their comfort over ours. Meaning, even when the fridge is empty, breakfast must be served.

Our reactions to brutality, whether violent or nonviolent, altruistic or vengeful, will be what gets printed in the newspaper, manufactured to appear as the epicenter of the matter, the headline. Politicians will often frame our response to brutalization, especially if it is militant, as the rationale behind their latest sordid policy, the reason why the earth spins on its axis. That we were brutalized at all is an ancillary factoid, tangential to our conduct and disposition. Consider mainstream media and the so-called international community treating the events of Octo-

---

* More on that later.

† Ahmed Alnaouq is a Palestinian journalist from Gaza and cofounder of We Are Not Numbers.

‡ In a later conversation, Ahmed told me that the number now is much higher than twenty-one. "I've honestly stopped counting," he said.

A LIFE IN CROSS-EXAMINATION 81

ber 7 as though they were the genesis of "the conflict." Consider the podiums, consider the bookshelves.

In 2009, Israeli soldiers killed, at once, a man's three daughters during an incursion into the Gaza Strip. This father then wrote a book titled *I Shall Not Hate*. In the catalog description of the book, before ever mentioning the author's slain children, the publisher, I assume, prepares the reader by articulating that this father is "a Harvard-trained" physician who "has devoted his life to medicine and reconciliation between Israelis and Palestinians . . . crossing the lines in the sand that divide Israelis and Palestinians for most of his life," treating "patients on both sides of the line," and that he is "a humanitarian" who sees "education for women as the way forward in the Middle East." Then came the daughters. After that, the reader is reassured once more, "Instead of seeking revenge or sinking into hatred," he "called for the people in the region to start talking to each other."

This bereaved man is Harvard-trained, that bereaved man has a heart of gold. A cruel joke: their bereavement is beside the question. The men offer consolation instead of receiving it, and the voyeurs at these televised funerals offer their conditional condolences in return. Once again, it is only through defanging that the Palestinian can communicate and narrativize. No more than a marginal narrative, but a narrative nonetheless, the story of the Palestinian as human *like you and me* is a story that has sought to resituate the Palestinian in a world where he exists without narrative, or, to be rigorous, a world where he is not self-authored and rather preceded by other people's definitions. Is this because of our alleged inability, "since [Ibn Sina] and Ibn

Khaldun" to produce "a theory of mind"?[3] Is it because "we have no known Einsteins, no Chagall, no Freud or Rubinstein" who would have otherwise protected us from infamy with "a legacy of glorious achievements"?[4] Or is there an answer slightly more sophisticated than pathetic self-flagellation?

The definitions that populate our notorieties are riven with mythology and paranoia. And often our words, in response, are a balm—even a strong dose of lithium. The elites and elitists in our ranks, even well-meaning allies, tell themselves (before they can convince the public) *Palestinians are just like you and me*: gentle fathers who love their wives, who have, contrary to popular belief, dogs (not cattle) as pets and a bone to pick with herd mentality, which, as we know, plagues the Arab mind. Palestinians can be their doppelgängers: "ferociously literate, well-dressed"[5] impersonators of civility. We relate to the elites, playing a little Beethoven, drinking a little wine, having a little premarital sex.* And if we are not Americans or Europeans in our mirrors, we must be exceptional to overcome that fact. We take the food out of our mouths to feed you. If it is not your spitting image in our reflection, we transform into superhumans who are as generous as a giving tree, as forgiving as God himself.

What is talked about as "relatability" is nothing more than ethnocentrism: if I am incomparable to your characteristics then I am indiscernible, and my opacity makes me not only inferior but disposable.[6] And those who are described in exceptional

---

* Mother, I have never.

A LIFE IN CROSS-EXAMINATION 83

terms—the bereaved who forgive killers, the insulted who do not retort—are promised a mirage that leaves the thirsty parched.

I remember picking up a copy of *I Shall Not Hate* in a bookshop on Jerusalem's Salah al-Din Street sometime in 2012. The story felt familiar. I could not recall whether I had heard this specific story or another equally devastating one. And I could not fathom the pain this father must have felt when the news broke against his back, the pain he must feel anytime he has to relive those moments. Still, when I pictured him in my mind, he had Abd el-Hadi's face and my father's. Amicable, agreeable, able to conjure a feast in the middle of a famine.

I must have been thirteen or fourteen years old at the time, trying to decipher, with broken English, the blurb on the back cover, then pausing to stare at the title, displayed in big, bold, block letters. *I SHALL NOT HATE.* I remember thinking, What if he did hate those who killed his daughters? What then?

84   PERFECT VICTIMS

MACHIAVELLIAN, ORWELLIAN, KAFKAESQUE, AND whatnot. History has a habit of transforming nouns into adjectives and, in that process, stripping them of a million layers of meaning. Perhaps that is the afterlife. One's ultimate destiny is to have their name in the end signify *one thing*, their complex life becomes a simple bullet point in people's memory.

Back in London, at the table in the pub, a friend, a British left-wing journalist, described Ahmed's response to the killing of his whole family apart from two sisters as "so human." I don't think he gave his word choice much thought. His politics are sound, his track record proves it, and he does not hesitate to look us in the eye. Remarks like these just happen to be part of an activist lexicon. It is not so much that he misspoke. Rather, he acted on the contrapuntal impulse to resituate us in the category from which we have been violently excluded: humanity. Ahmed is indeed one of the kindest, most principled persons I have ever met. A paragon of patience, an awe-inspiring model of composure. But "human" is not an adjective, certainly not a compliment.

To some, the fixation on one misused adjective might sound like an unimportant game of semantics. But one's understanding of words defines one's relationship with them, a relationship of profound importance, capable of shaping one's worldview and modulating one's actions. Language, as such, is the medium of knowledge, and knowledge—as the adage goes—is power, political power, the "psychological relation between those who exercise it and those over whom it is exercised."[7] In accepting this adage, one is able to recognize the source of the seemingly self-inflicted wounds that riddle our rhetoric, the origin of the memorized preludes that precede our statements: the colonizer's domination over discourse.

Our enemies employ what Mourid Barghouti calls "a simple linguistic trick" to turn the world on its head: they fail to mention what came first and start their story from "secondly."[8] "Start your story with 'secondly,'" Barghouti writes, "and the arrows of the Red Indians are the original criminals, and the guns of the white men are entirely the victim. It is enough to start with 'secondly' for the anger of the black man against the white to be barbarous" as opposed to justified or even admirable.[9] The peril of this supposedly inconsequential language game is revealed in its ability to obscure reality. However, more importantly, language possesses a transformative potential to elucidate, demystify, repair, liberate, and rival; to infiltrate consciousnesses and permeate into collective action; to "support the weight of a civilization."[10] Language, if we can dominate it, can turn our anonymous whispers back into thunderous declarations.

That Ahmed decided (or felt pressured) to declare, mere days after the occupation shelled his family to death, his rejection of antisemitism speaks volumes about him. Volumes for others to discern. I have little desire to interrogate his motives. I am confident they are pure rather than calculated quid pro quo. More than the individual himself, we need to understand the external and internal pressures exerted on the individual, the global context that necessitates such behavior.

How have we allowed the world to demand of us hospitality even in hunger? What is it that makes an untimely and out-of-place disavowal of bigotry seem like a crucial part of an

86   PERFECT VICTIMS

obituary? Is disproving libel the sole reason we roam this earth? We talk about the racism that follows the Palestinian's name, particularly its manifestations in policy and procedure, but we should also consider its psychic cost. Do we understand the impact such aspersions have on the Palestinian's psyche? How does spending a life in cross-examination influence our gaze? How does it guide our interactions and relationships? Have we, in our efforts to disown the legacy of the terrorist, reared settlers in our subconscious?

Ahmed's gesture of goodwill may be graceful and generous. Superhuman, even, all things considered. But it cannot be classified as "human," because it asks too much of him and of us all. Or, to be precise, it asks too much of those of us who aspire to "become human." As such, the complex, multifarious condition that is humanity, as it exists in our consciousness, is mutilated into a reductive adjective that conveys a state of being that is so unattainably angelic, so infuriatingly perfect.

This mandate, to be human in this way, imposes an inordinate burden on those mourning their slain loved ones. Grieving a loss is bad enough; doing it under the panopticon of public scrutiny is abasing.* Not only that, but Palestinians are tasked with articulating their grief under the literal surveillance of the settler state and its mercenaries. And much like the way the col-

---

* For Palestinians, this surveillance is both physical (there is a settler setting up yet another lamppost in my neighborhood and another settler lurking in the software of my phone) and figurative (the crowds before which we have been trained to perform).

ony passes laws *meant* to criminalize what it deems undesirable, transgressive symptoms of our grief, its mercs establish institutional policies to suppress and punish them. Take a look at the academy, for example. A valedictorian, minoring in "resistance to genocide," was banned from delivering her graduation speech for fear she would reference genocide.[11] A hospital fired a nurse it had honored days earlier with an "award for her 'exceptional' work with bereaving women who had lost children during pregnancy or childbirth" during this genocide.[12] Students all around the globe set up encampments in protest of the genocide, and university administrators responded in ways that can only be described as draconian. There I go, using nouns as adjectives.

IN A HOTEL ROOM IN BERKELEY, CALIFORNIA, I recounted Ahmed's story to a friend. Or, I recounted to a friend what I believed Ahmed's story to be. In reality, it was not even a chapter in it but a mere scene, a scene to which I assigned my own interpretation. What is it that drives us to turn people into allegories? And what allegory will I forge from this conversation?

I think it was raining when we arrived at the UC Berkeley encampment.* We just happened to be on campus for an event that was planned months in advance, which we ended up cutting short before escorting attendees to the encampment. I was asked to speak to the protesting students in hopes that I would raise morale. I told them, without much eloquence, that they would be smeared and maligned no matter what and that I hoped "victory" would come from a public university instead of an Ivy League. The latter, I argued, receive a disproportionate amount of press coverage. Someone had explained to me that homeless people had been sleeping in the students' tents after their own encampment had been depopulated and destroyed by the city and its police force. I thought such a detail needed to be editorialized (to attract media attention, of course). The tent cities on campuses were "heaven on earth," as one student at the Columbia University encampment had told me. Utopias where the hungry eat and the homeless shelter, microcosms of a future Palestine where "Jews, Muslims, and Christians pray uninterrupted."

---

* The Free Palestine Encampment at University of California, Berkeley, posed four demands, including that the university divest from companies funding and supporting Israeli apartheid and genocide.

A LIFE IN CROSS-EXAMINATION   89

In the hotel room, as I recounted "Ahmed's story" to my friend, I mentioned his voluntary disavowal of antisemitism and the conversation that followed in the pub, a conversation that had haunted me for months. What got under my skin was not only the demand that we exhibit an extraordinarily docile disposition in the face of colonial brutality but the implication that Ahmed's contempt would have disqualified him as a victim. It was also the strange fact that the hatred we supposedly possess, lurking within our hearts, receives more concern than the nuclear arsenal of our colonizers. In my friend's perspective, however, Ahmed was not conceding to colonial demands; rather, he was simply behaving as Palestinians do. Ahmed's virtuous approach personifies Palestinian culture, which in turn is exemplary of the overall nature of the native. We simply have a "different value system" than the colonizer, she said to me, we have a different character. I told her that was the poet in her.

She reminded me that Indigenous nations in what is now known as the United States gave the arriving settlers food, and the settlers in turn offered them smallpox and genocide. Those respective actions are indicative of traits that are innate to the settler and the native, or so the argument goes. "The intrinsic nature of having no home training," she called it. Yosef Weitz came to mind and all the ways he resembled Christopher Columbus. "By and large there is a different approach to the world and way of seeing the world that allows us to move differently. Our flaws are different," she said. "Our flaws haven't led us to the position of indoctrinating and systematizing the worst parts of ourselves to subjugate other people." We are simply cognitively different beings. Or, in Césaire's words, "A nation which colonizes . . . is already a sick civilization."[13] Perhaps, then, it isn't poetry. Perhaps Ahmed's actions prove Césaire's prophecy that "every denial of justice . . . every punitive expedition" brings us closer to "the value of our old societies." Societies that were "communal . . . anti-capitalist [and] democratic."[14]

But if it were true that the native is "fraternal," the settler "morally diseased,"[15] then what do we make of the thieving and the treacherous among us, the stingy and the spiteful? Do they not deserve freedom? And what about the murderers and rapists in our cities? The greedy and the corrupt? Are their crimes products of mere circumstance—poverty, colonialism, racism—and without such circumstances our societies would be utopian? Or are certain violences intrinsic to human nature? How does this narrative describe me? How does it explain my rage toward the settlers who live in my home? Are my sentiments so freakishly abnormal that they abandon the suggested moral authority of the native and mimic the vindictive, hateful ways of the colonizer?

I will not question the fact that colonialism has pillaged and underdeveloped the world. Nor the fact that imperialism has incapacitated our societies. And, though tempting, I will not ask whether we, as "non-European civilizations," have consistently embodied such noble characteristics. History is fickle and so is identity. What I will ask instead is this: Why do the values of our societies, past and present, matter in those debates?

If we are assessing a certain ideological project (say, capi-

A LIFE IN CROSS-EXAMINATION 91

talism, Zionism, so on), why not judge it based on how it materially manifests rather than on the perceived attributes of its subjects? Zionism is best defined by its material manifestations—Zionism is what Zionism does. When Zionism's most recent manifestation is genocide, what difference does it make whether the encampments protesting this genocide are utopias of coexistence? What difference does it make how the grieving grieve? Curating the native as "respectable" is a misplaced priority because it redirects critical scrutiny away from the colonizer, which in turn neglects the innate injustice of the colonial project. This misplaced focus insinuates that the oppressed must earn what they are already entitled to: liberty, dignity, and basic rights. Otherwise, if the native is not "respectable," slavery and subjugation would be necessarily applicable, rather than morally reprehensible. Nothing reveals more about the colonizer's psyche than these arrogant expectations.

Let us consider again the violence visited upon Ahmed, the insurmountable, suffocating sorrow one is bound to feel after a loss of such devastating proportion: twenty-one of your kin, slain at once. What becomes of you when words no longer suffice, when "sorrow" loses its potency and when "suffocation" loosens its grip? What becomes of the 2.3 million Palestinians in Gaza, whose calendars are marked by routine bombardments? What are the mental and muscular consequences of being forced to transform a taxi into a hearse? What becomes of the nurse whose shift is interrupted by the arrival of her husband's corpse on a stretcher? What about the father wandering with what remains of his son in two plastic bags? What happens to him after all of this death, once he is alone and away from the cameras? What kind of man will the boy carrying his brother's limbs in a bag grow up to be? Does it matter whether he emerges as Abd el-Hadi or as Abu Obaida? Does it make Zionism any less indefensible?

So I ask again: What if our perfect victims do in fact despise those who have killed their families? Then what? Let me ask the most exaggerated, extreme version of this question: What if, after a Star-of-David-clad soldier of the self-proclaimed "Jewish state" killed your loved ones in cold blood, you began to obsessively, irrationally hate Jews, all Jews, wherever they may be? Then what? Does your venomous sentiment undermine your status as a victim? Does it rewrite history to absolve the soldier of his sins? Does it justify the crime?

A LIFE IN CROSS-EXAMINATION 93

SEVENTEEN YEARS AFTER ABD EL-HADI FED THE NAVY SEALS BREAKFAST, Taha Muhammad Ali returned to him in a new poem titled "Abd el-Hadi the Fool." The protagonist, a fictional character inspired by certain men from the poet's depopulated village, Saffuriyya, "and the hapless movie fat man Oliver Hardy,"[16] was now speaking for himself, no longer represented by an attorney pleading before a jury. "I was naive," Abd el-Hadi confesses. "I loved horses and poetry / I dreamed of a meal / that would last forever . . . I was a fool." But at the height of the First Intifada, "after the springs were buried alive, / after the watercourses' destruction," he returned to the page militant, politicized, and "charged with a sharpened hatred."[17]

> I want to burn down the world
> I want to stab it
> in its soft belly
> I want to dismember the world
> after drowning it*

In the published translation of this poem, the above stanza is printed in the past tense.[18] I have elected to alter the tenses so that they more accurately reflect the original Arabic poem. In English, Abd el-Hadi's desire to burn down the world is presented as though it is already long gone, an artifact of another

---

* "أتمنى حرق العالم!

أتمنى طعنه / في بطنه

أتمنى تفكيك الكون / بعد إغراقه"

94   PERFECT VICTIMS

time. Perhaps this was a stylistic or a sonic choice, or it was meant to diffuse any tension the anglophone reader might feel reading through an Arab man's violent fantasies. But this is not a poem of repentance, with Abd el-Hadi reflecting on his now-resolved past hatred. Rather, the poet offers his protagonist an arena to contend with the multiplicity of his sentiments and their contradictory nature.

The Palestinian's individual responses to the man-made catastrophes inflicted upon them are only indicative of the Palestinian's disposition as an individual, whether they are our reactions to being forcibly expelled from our villages and towns or our reactions to the aerial bombardment of our families. These reactions do not change who bears guilt, nor do they imply a standard to be obeyed. To call a certain reaction to injustice "human" is to imply that others are inhuman, subhuman, brutish. No one has the right to make that call. There is no uniform way to grieve the killing of your loved ones. Sometimes it is graceful, other times it is vengeful. Sometimes it is muffled, other times it is explosive. Sometimes one only dreams of revenge, and other times one pursues it. I might argue that the probable response to genocide is rage and hatred, whether rational or irrational, but grief is a lot more complicated and contradictory than this position. Abd el-Hadi continues, "my greatest apostasy / is this:"

> no sooner does the laughter
> of a child reach me,
> or I happen upon
> a sobbing stream,

> no sooner do I see
> a flower wilting,
> or notice a fine-looking woman,
> than I am stunned
> and abandoned by everything,
> and nothing of me remains,
> except
> Abd el-Hadi the fool!*

And there are many Abd el-Hadis, all around, who can forgive or forget, or at least be momentarily distracted, who embrace "the righteous and the wicked alike" and greet "the victim and the hangman as one."[19] But there are also people, everywhere, even within Abd el-Hadi himself, who want to dismember the world and set it ablaze.

They see the thieves banging their gavels and the liars boasting of their journalism degrees. They know their pockets are picked to pay for the butcher's knives. And they have seen those knives at work, stabbing their siblings, slicing their flesh. There are people who have contempt for the world that greets a nurse with her husband's corpse on a stretcher, the world that forces

---

*

"لكنْ / ردّتي الكبرى / أنّني
ما إن تبلغني / ضحكة طفلٍ
أو أصادف / جدولًا ينتحبُ،
ما إن أشاهدُ / زهرةً ذابلةً
أو أرى إمرأةٍ جميلةً —
حتى أُصعقُ / يغادرني / كل شيءٍ
ولا يبقى منّي / سِوى / عبد الهادي الأهبلْ!"

a boy to carry his brother's limbs in a bag. I am one of those people. And I am grateful for my disdain, for it is dignifying; it reminds me that I am human.

▼

5.   *tropes and drones*

> *One does not wish, in short, to be told by an*
> *American Jew that his suffering is as great as*
> *the American Negro's suffering. It isn't, and one*
> *knows that it isn't from the very tone in which*
> *he assures you that it is.*
>
> —James Baldwin[1]

WHEN WE WERE GROWING UP IN OCCUPIED JERU-SALEM, the people seeking to expel us from our neighborhood were Jewish, and their organizations often had "Jewish" in their name.[2] So were the people who stole our home, scattered our furniture in the street, and burned my baby sister's crib. The judges banging their gavels in favor of our expulsion were also Jewish, and so were the lawmakers whose laws systematized our dispossession. On some afternoons, I came home from school to find busloads of Jewish tourists in our front yard, pointing at us like animals at an auction, spitting American expletives in our faces. Some mornings, young-looking settlers would be shuckling in our garden, in their kippahs and tefillin. Others were older and secular: they wore khakis and sandals and did

98   PERFECT VICTIMS

not pray much. Every couple of months, they would knock at our door and smirk as they handed my grandmother expulsion orders and court summons.

The bureaucrat issuing and revoking our blue ID cards was a Jew, and I especially despised him because a stroke of his pen stood between my father and my father's great-great-grandfather's city. As for the soldiers who were frisking us to check for those IDs, some of them were Druze, some Muslim, most of them Jewish, and all of them, according to my grandmother, were "godless bastards." Those who administered the rifles and handcuffs, those who wrote the meticulous and murderous urban plans were—you guessed it.

This was no secret. We grew up under the rule of the self-proclaimed "Jewish state." Israeli politicians have exhausted this line, and their international peers nodded along, blurring, invisibilizing, effacing the line between synagogue and state. This was the Jews' only homeland, their tiny haven in a hostile neighborhood. The army declared itself a Jewish army and marched under what it has called a Jewish flag. Jerusalem city councilmen boasted of "tak[ing] house after house" on our street.[3] They stood at our doorstep and told us, "You are against the Bible. . . . God says this area belongs to the Jewish people."[4] Knesset members sang similar tunes of Jewish supremacy. And such legislators were not fringe or far-right: the Israeli Nation-State Law explicitly enshrines "Jewish settlement" as a "national value . . . to encourage and promote."[5] When the law was challenged, its legality was upheld by the Israeli supreme court, which ruled it does not negate the settler state's "democratic character."*

Though the settler colony's Jewish character was no secret, we were still instructed to treat it as such, sometimes by our parents, other times by well-meaning solidarity activists. We were instructed to ignore the Star of David on the Israeli flag and to distinguish Jews from Zionists with surgical precision. It did not matter that their boots were on our necks, and that their bullets and batons bruised us. Our statelessness and homelessness were trivial; what mattered was how we *spoke* about our keepers, not the conditions they kept us under—burglarized, blockaded, surrounded by col-

---

* The fingerprints of the supreme court are all over the Israeli government's settler-colonial enterprises and apartheid regime, not just the Nation-State Law. The court repeatedly supported the legality of the "family reunification law" that robs thousands of Palestinian couples holding different legal statuses of "the basic right of being together as a family." (See Al Tahhan, "'Devastating.'") In 2006, the court rejected two challenges to the route of the Israeli separation-and-annexation wall, allowing the construction of the barrier on Palestinian-owned lands in occupied Jerusalem, including a cemetery. In its entire history, the supreme court has never once granted a petition to cancel an administrative detention order. Instead, it has served as a rubber stamp for the Israeli military's draconian policy of indefinite detention without trial. Additionally, in 2018, it ruled that the Israeli Security Agency's guidelines for the use of "special" and "physical means of interrogation" (i.e., torture) are legitimate in "ticking bomb" circumstances. (See Shoughry-Badarne, "Torture in Israel.") During the brutal crackdown on the Great March of Return, the court ruled that the occupation forces' use of lethal force against Palestinian demonstrators was "legitimate self-defense." (See Erakat, "Sovereign Right to Kill.") The supreme court has also repeatedly upheld the long-running Israeli policy of withholding the corpses of Palestinians and using them as "bargaining chips," and it has authorized the army's restrictions on Palestinian funerals, playing a pivotal role in institutionalizing the Zionist regime's practices of necroviolence. See El-Kurd, "Israeli Protesters."

onies and military outposts—or the fact that they kept us at all.

Language was more of a minefield than the border that separated the occupied Golan Heights from the rest of Syria, and we, children at the time, were expected to hop around the land mines, hoping we would not accidentally step on an explosive trope that would discredit us. Using the wrong words has the magical ability to make objects disappear; the boots, bullets, batons, and bruises all become invisible if you say the wrong words, in jest or in fury. Even more dangerously, believing in the wrong things rendered you deserving of this brutality. Citizenship, self-determination, and the right to movement were not the sole privileges robbed from us; simple ignorance was a luxury as well.

TROPES AND DRONES   101

WE UNDERSTAND FROM A YOUNG AGE that, as Palestinians, the semantic violence we supposedly practice with our words dwarfs the decades of systemic and material violence enacted against us by the self-proclaimed "Jewish state." A drone is one thing, but a trope—a trope is *unacceptable*. We learn to internalize the muzzle.*

So, I heeded these calls—what else is a ten-year-old supposed to do?—and I studied Hitler and the Holocaust, and I mastered all of the stereotypes: the noses, the poisoned wells, the bankers, the vampires, the snakes, and the lizards (I found out about the octopus† later in life). I also learned to riddle my speech with disclaimers and disavowals when speaking to diplomats visiting our zoo of a neighborhood. The settlers squatting in our home had to be the secondary point of my presentation, second to an effusive denunciation of global antisemitism. And when my octogenarian grandmother addressed those foreign visitors, I "corrected" her mid-sentence whenever she described the Jewish settlers in our house as, well, Jewish.

A decade and some years later and not much has changed. The busloads of American Jews still pilgrimage to our humble abode. My run-ins with the police are still as Hebrew as they are unpleasant. The boot remains, so do the bullets and batons.

---

* After/inspired by Saidiya V. Hartman's quote: "The whip was not to be abandoned; rather, it was to be internalized." Hartman, *Scenes of Subjection*, 140.

† This trope traces back to a Nazi-era cartoon depicting Jews as an octopus with tentacles wrapped around the globe to symbolize the enduring stereotype of Jewish world domination.

And I would be remiss not to mention the innovative genius of the AI-powered robot firearms added to the "Jewish state's" arsenal in recent years.[6] The government titles its decades-long project to expel Palestinians from the Galilee as "the Judaization of the Galilee," and its quasi-institutions do the same. As for the council members who promised and often succeeded to take "house after house" in Sheikh Jarrah, Silwan, and the Old City, they routinely march in our towns with megaphones and flags, chanting, "We want Nakba now."

The judges still bang their gavels to ensure the continuation of this Nakba, still rule in favor of Jewish supremacy. And, despite disagreeing with the supreme court on various issues, parliamentarians legislate in accordance with that supremacist attitude. Some openly state the fact that Jewish life is simply more important than our freedom. Sometimes they're even nice enough to apologize to Arab TV presenters as they deliver them these hard truths.[7] A decade and some years later, the status quo ante remains current. And we—how my heart breaks for us—we continue dancing among the land mines. We continue betting on morality and humanity, as they bet on their guns.

IN AUGUST 2023, SIXTEEN ISRAELI POLICE OFFI-CERS TURNED OFF THEIR BODY CAMERAS and branded, as in *physically etched*, the Star of David into the cheek of 22-year-old Orwa Sheikh Ali, a young man they arrested from the Shuʿfat refugee camp in occupied Jerusalem.[8] Two weeks after that, MEMRI, a media watch group cofounded by a former Israeli military intelligence officer, disseminated previously broadcast footage of Mahmoud Abbas, the president of the Palestinian Authority, stating that Europeans "fought [the Jews] because of their social role" and "usury" and "not because of their religion."[9] When Mr. President isn't a mur-derer and a collaborator, he is pseudo-intellectual. In response, a group of renowned Palestinian academics, many of whom I admire and respect, published an open letter "unequivocally condemn[ing]"—guess what?—Abbas's "morally and politi-cally reprehensible comments."[10]

Some could call their joint statement a strategic move to negate the belief that Palestinians are born bigoted. Others may say it represents what having a consistent moral code looks like. I'm certain some signatories believe our so-called moral author-ity makes it incumbent upon us to deplore historical revisionism "vis-à-vis the Holocaust,"[11] that we ought to lead by example in rejecting all forms of racism, no matter how rhetorical, so on and so forth. After all, Palestinians, especially in the diaspora, have spent decades toiling to create spaces where they can be anti-Zionist and maintain alliances with progressive American and European Jews, who would have been insulted and alarmed by Abbas's remarks.

104   PERFECT VICTIMS

Whatever the rationale, when I read the letter, I felt a sense of déjà vu. Here we are, caught in a discursive crisis once more, frantically denying our culpability in crimes we have not committed.* I felt a sadness engulf me when I recognized, again, that these are the terms of engagement in the West, that this is what necessitates a coordinated campaign. While the signatories of the letter (some of whom have criticized the Palestinian Authority since its inception) did decry the "PA's increasingly authoritarian and draconian rule," and while they made note of the "Western and pro-Israel forces" supporting Abbas's expired presidential mandate, neither of those components served as the catalyst for what appeared to be the first joint statement condemning Mahmoud Abbas.† The letter did not spell his collaboration with the Zionist regime as its headline, nor his brutalization of protesters and political prisoners, let alone the murder of Nizar Banat‡—

---

* One issue is that the letter inadvertently establishes Mahmoud Abbas—a dictator whom many of the signatories have been criticizing since before I was born—as a representative of the Palestinian People. If we are in agreement that the Palestinian Authority is a subcontractor for the Israeli occupation, why are we obliged to publicly disown statements made by its officials?

† I want to make clear that I do not make any attempts to undermine anyone's contributions to our struggle, even if I disagree with their tactics. I, however, find it ironic that when the upwardly mobile and institutionally backed among us criticize the makeshift tactics employed by the crushed classes, they are seldom accused of "fragmenting the movement" or "airing out our dirty laundry." The idea that criticism is "divisive" is reductive and intellectually lazy. Honest, unrehearsed conversations are crucial to building resilient movements.

‡ Nizar Banat (1978–2021) was a Palestinian political dissident born in Durra in the occupied West Bank. He was a famous activist, an outspoken critic of the PA, and a member of the Freedom and Dignity List, which was formed

offenses that are far more deplorable than historical revisionism. The catalyst here was words. Mere words. And it always is.
Again, a drone is one thing, but a trope is off-limits.

The strategy of defending ourselves, often preemptively,
against the baseless charge of antisemitism has historically
brought us closer to it. And, more than that, such an impulse
inadvertently elevates the history of Jewish suffering—which is
certainly studied, if not honored—above our present-day suffering, a suffering that is denied and disputed, despite being relentlessly televised.*

And what a burdensome impulse! Not only do we live in
fear of death and displacement at the hands of a colonialism that
professes *itself* as Jewish, not only are our people bombarded by
an army that marches under what *it* claims is the Jewish flag, and
not only do Israeli politicians over-enunciate the Jewishness of
their operations; we are also told to disregard the Star of David
soaring on their flag, the Star of David they carve into our skin.

But this is a tale as old as "the conflict" itself. And like that,
generations of Palestinians have worked to dispel the conflation
between Zionism and Judaism. In his handwritten transcript of

---

to contest the cancelation 2021 Palestinian Legislative Council elections by
PA leader Mahmoud Abbas. On June 24, 2021, Banat was arrested and beat-
en to death by PA security forces.

* Ironically, both the joint letter and Abbas's speech sought to distance themselves from antisemitism. At the start of the clip, Abbas wanted to "clarify"
that he said what he said regarding "European Jews . . . hav[ing] nothing to
do with Semitism" because we ought to "know who we should accuse of being our enemy."

a speech he gave in Cairo in October 1948, Palestinian educator Khalil Sakakini struck through a fragment of a sentence that read "the fighting between Arabs and Jews," to replace it with "the fighting between us and the invaders." Palestinian academics, the Institute for Palestine Studies, and the PLO's Palestine Research Center (which the Israeli regime looted and bombed repeatedly in 1980s) have dedicated articles, books, and volumes to the study of antisemitism—its European roots and its manifestations, European or otherwise—and its conflation with anti-Zionism.

The Palestinian People have consistently made it crystal clear that our enemy is Zionism, an ideology of dispossession, an expansionist and racist settler-colonial enterprise. Zionism, not Jews. Our capacity to produce such distinction is admirable and impressive, considering the heavy-handedness with which Zionism attempts to synonymize itself with Judaism. However, this distinction is not our responsibility, and, personally, it is not my priority. A Palestinian's perceived resentment doesn't have the backing of a Knesset to codify it into law. Tropes aren't drones, nor can one convert conspiracy theories into nuclear weapons. We are past the early 1900s. Things are different, power has shifted. Words are not murder.

TROPES AND DRONES

IN THE DAYS BETWEEN THE SIXTEEN POLICEMEN BRANDING A MAN'S FACE with the Star of David and the release of the intelligentsia's joint letter,[12] an Israeli soldier killed Islam Nofel, a disabled young man, near a military checkpoint in Qalqilya;[13] another shot a child, fifteen-year-old Abd Amer Al-Zaghal, in the head in Silwan;[14] a young man named Muhammad Abu Asab, previously shot by soldiers raiding the Balata refugee camp, died of his injuries;[15] a sniper shot Ameed Al-Jaghoub in the head in Beita;[16] seventeen-year-old Othman Abu Khoruj was shot and killed south of Jenin;[17] one more young man, Ata Yasser Ata Mousa, succumbed to his wounds following an invasion of the Jenin refugee camp;[18] families of Palestinians whose corpses are held by the Occupation authorities marched with empty caskets in Nablus;[19] a soldier killed a boy near Hebron;[20] police executed fourteen-year-old Khaled Samer Fadel al-Zaanin in Sheikh Jarrah to the applause of hundreds of settlers;[21] the police then tear-gassed his family in Beit Hanina;[22] a man was killed after ramming soldiers in Beit Sira, killing one;[23] in the north of Jericho, a teenager was killed and a soldier was injured in a gun battle;[24] a soldier shot Abdul Rahim Fayez Ghannam in the head in Tubas, killing him.[25] This is only the very tip of the iceberg.

Which of these caused far-reaching debate within Palestinian circles in the diaspora? None. There was noise concerning Itamar Ben-Gvir* suggesting on television that Jewish life is more

---

* Ben-Gvir's résumé reads almost like a caricature of itself. A lawyer for two of the settlers who participated in the 2015 firebombing of a Palestinian household that killed all but one of its members, he has represented a "'Who's

108 PERFECT VICTIMS

important than Palestinian freedom,˙ less noise about the carving of the Star of David, and, of course, Mahmoud Abbas received the noisiest reaction of all.

Those examples deal with aesthetics. Optics. Ben-Gvir's statements were factual and true: Jewish life *is* worth more than ours under Israeli rule. But it was his explicit oration, not the institutionalized policies that have made his racist remarks the material reality on the ground, that triggered outrage. Even the physical deformation of a Palestinian's face was only of note because of what the etching *symbolized*, not the etching itself. Had the soldiers cut inconspicuous lines on his cheek, it would not have garnered any attention at all,

---

Who' of suspects in Jewish terror cases and hate crimes." (Maltz, "Lawyer for Jewish Terrorists.") He has repeatedly helped organize the notoriously racist "flag march," during which thousands of Israeli settlers march through the Old City of Jerusalem—some shouting "Death to Arabs"—celebrating the 1967 occupation. He has pulled his gun on two Palestinian parking lot workers. He has demanded the expulsion of "disloyal Arabs" to other Arab countries during his—very successful—election campaign. He also has a habit of attempting to storm the hospital rooms of hunger-striking Palestinian prisoners. Until 2020, he proudly hung in his living room a portrait of Baruch Goldstein, the American turned settler turned mass murderer who massacred twenty-nine Palestinians as they prayed in the Ibrahimi Mosque in Hebron in 1994. But most important: Ben-Gvir is a settler in Hebron.

* Ben-Gvir said, "The right of me, my wife, and kids to travel around the West Bank is more important than that of the Arabs." He then told reporters: "It is simple, the right to life supersedes the right to free movement." He followed up with a tweet: "I said yesterday on a TV broadcast that the right of Jews to live and not be murdered in terror attacks prevails over the right of Arabs in [the West Bank] to travel on the roads without security restrictions."

something I say with confidence because such violence is as frequent as its coverage is sparse. As for Palestinian death, it is quotidian and negligible. If we're lucky, our martyrs are tallied up in sums on the pages of end-of-year reports. So-called revisionism, on the other hand, warrants a universal cacophony of condemnation.

Here is where I stand. There is a Jew who lives, by force, in half of my home in Jerusalem, and he does so by "divine decree," in the name of the Jewish people. Many others reside, by force, on Palestinian land and in Palestinian houses, while their actual owners languish in refugee camps. It is not my fault that they are Jewish. I have zero interest in apologizing for centuries-old tropes created by Europeans, when millions of us confront real, tangible oppression, living behind cement walls, or under siege, or in exile, and living with woes too expansive to summarize. I am tired of the impulse to preemptively distance myself from something of which I am not guilty, and particularly tired of the constant burden to prove that I am not inherently bigoted. I'm tired of the pearl-clutching pretense that should such animosity exist, its existence would be inexplicable and rootless, of the academics and the intellectuals punching down on the unfiltered among us. Most of all, I am tired of the false equivalence between semantic "violence" and systemic violence: only one party in this "conflict" is actively engaged in the intentional and systematic attempted eradication of an entire population.

I know this chapter is within itself a minefield. It will be taken out of context, disseminated and disfigured, but I will never be a perfect victim. There is no escaping being accused of antisemitism. It is a losing battle and, more importantly, a glaring red herring. And it is time we reevaluate this tactic. There are better things to do: we have coffins to carry; we have kin in Israeli mortuary chambers that we must bury.

6.   mein kampf *in the playroom*

If the fool speaks, do not answer.
—al-Shafi'

THE ISRAELI PRESIDENT SAT IN FRONT OF A MENO-RAH when he showed the BBC "something exclusive" his infantry had found "in a children's living room"[1] in northern Gaza: a copy of *Mein Kampf.* And in Arabic, no less. It was proof of "the real war" Isaac Herzog and his colonymen are waging, a war not against children but against their reprehensible taste in literature.

Naturally, this "children's living room" had been "turned into a military operation base." And there it was, hiding in plain sight: a work usually locked away in underground vaults, behind laser sensors and panic buttons. What an omen. After all, this was the book that "led to the worst atrocity of humankind, which the British fought against," he told the British anchor, almost admonishing her. "The terrorist" who owned the book, or borrowed it from the children's commune, "even marked [it up]," Herzog alerted us, his voice now solemn and no longer grating—a sobering moment, I think. Yes, terrorists with pens. "He wrote notes! He marked. He marked and learned and learned again and again," Herzog exclaimed.[2] A paradigm shift: the terrorists know how to read.

It was the talk of the town, and every jester had a joke. State-sponsored propagandists and unpaid mouthpieces alike rushed to weaponize this "finding" as a legitimate pretext for genocide, as there was no other explanation: the Palestinians were plotting the extermination of the Jews; thus they must be exterminated. And in response to the clowns and their circus, our impulse was to meticulously debunk Herzog's claims.* *The book was planted there! Look at the copy he's holding, it's pristine! Those pages have never been flipped through. Besides, there are copies of* Mein Kampf *on the shelves of Haifa University! And Tel Aviv University! The person who owned the book was probably just curious and wanted to research the evil of Hitler! God forbid men have hobbies!*

But why is this our impulse? An extremely well-trained muscle is responsible for the refutation reflex, which has become an intrinsic part of the Palestinian body. The Zionist entity has for decades been planting weapons and manufacturing evidence, laying fruit knives next to assassinated schoolgirls. But since

---

* In another instance, at the Munich Security Conference, Herzog held up a plastic-wrapped copy of a book titled *The End of the Jews* and falsely claimed it was written by senior Hamas leader Mahmoud al-Zahar. Major international news outlets, including the *New York Post*, published the story without confirming its accuracy. The book was in fact written by an Egyptian author named Abu al-Fida Muhammad Aref. Centre for Combating Disinformation - Palestine, #*Palestine*.

MEIN KAMPF IN THE PLAYROOM 113

when is a book a weapon? When did it become incriminating evidence? Why do we have to meet absurdity with seriousness? Instead of succumbing to this annihilatory logic that renders us criminals of thought based on what we supposedly read or believe, why not say that *even if* that pristine copy of *Mein Kampf* was found in a children's playroom where it was read like a bedtime story, that does not give the Zionist regime, which occupies and colonizes our lands, the permission to exterminate us. Nothing in my character or on my bookshelf, even the horrid, should determine whether I live or die. Nothing in my ideology, even if it is inflammatory; nothing in my disposition, even if it is uncouth.

I once credulously believed that our testimonies would be considered credible only once we attained "respectability." Colonial logic gaslights us to believe that it is our shortcomings, not colonialism itself, that stand between us and liberation. And so we spend our years on a circuitous journey toward an impossible atonement. We accept starting the story at "Secondly." But in truth, and to state the obvious, nothing renders me killable. Before I threw the rock, they stole my land. Before I picked up the rifle, they shot my loved ones. Before I made the makeshift rocket, they put me in a cage. What I read cannot be used as a pretext to kill me, even if I filled my library with books written by psychopaths, interchangeably stacking copies of *Mein Kampf* and Hillary Clinton's *Hard Choices*.

PROPAGANDA IS A CHILDREN'S BOOK. Successful propagandists strive to create talking points that are simultaneously simplistic and incoherent. The overt simplicity invites an easy, enthusiastic repetition, which becomes a melody of sorts, transforming even the dim into leading singers in the choir. The incoherence invites ceaseless argumentation; the very point is to make you want to bang your head against the wall.

Hitler's manifesto in northern Gaza has everything in common with any other Zionist cliché: it is rooted in glaring logical fallacies. At first, it may seem shocking how a tale so ridiculous can be so potent and effective. But how many hours have you wasted defending against ad hominem attacks (*No, our men are gentle fathers!*) or assuaging the paranoias of strawman arguments (*No, "from the river to the sea" is not a secret call to genocide!*) or navigating slippery slopes (*No, a free Palestine will not lead to a second Holocaust!*) or pausing for red herrings (*No, there are no tunnels under the hospital!*) or appealing to authority (*Even the Israeli scholars agree that it is a genocide!*) or debunking equivocations (*No, anti-Zionism is not antisemitism!*)? The very quality of propaganda—illogic—is precisely its strongest suit, because it is a distraction.

Distraction from what? The focal point: colonialism, siege, military occupation. Our children's remains collected in shoeboxes, the torture our men endure in detention centers that can only be described as concentration camps, the women threatened with rape at gunpoint, the demolished homes, the demolished dreams, the generations robbed of a future, the people burnt alive in tents. And is there room for side conversations in the presence of burning flesh?

MEIN KAMPF IN THE PLAYROOM 115

Let me ask another question: Why do Israeli leaders peddle playground talk like "Israel has a right to exist" and "there is no 'P' in Arabic"?[23] Why would Netanyahu stand on an international stage and make the absurd, ahistorical claim that the Mufti of Jerusalem inspired the Holocaust?[24] Because the absurdity is the point of his diatribe—it provides his allies with a childish anthem for taunting us, and it tempts us into believing that the absurd can be fought with logical reasoning. Not all statements are made in good faith. Often, the impulse to debunk myths, the reflex to refute fabrications—whatever you want to call it—leads us to forget that propaganda is, by design, a diversion. "Even if" does not forget this fact; "even if" is a sobering refrain.

And "even if" remains logical. When confronted with the racist trope that Palestinian resistance fighters use civilians as human shields, it is tempting to pull up video footage of Israeli soldiers using our bodies for that exact reason,[5] or maps showing the Israeli military's headquarters situated in the heart of bustling, densely populated Tel Aviv. These, after all, are cogent retorts. But why accept the premise of the question in the first place? Even if the human shield allegations were true, why submit to a logic that argues it is acceptable to kill those classified as civilians if, hypothetically, "terrorists" hid behind them? If, say, a robber took your mother hostage and hid behind her, would the police officer on the scene be absolved of all responsibility if he decided to kill your mother to neutralize the robber?

I use the analogy of the robber and policeman consciously. Zionists have penned a narrative where they are a force for good, legitimately fighting off intruders. But the reality, of course, is the inverse. Colonialism is the robber and the policeman at once, committing the crime and legalizing it.

Zionists frame their systemic and policy-driven actions as a regrettable necessity, as if those actions are outside of their control, an inescapable fate in which we are forcing them to kill our children. This was Golda Meir's vile catchphrase, and it has reverberated ever since.* But Golda Meir could have spared our children. No one forced her. She chose to kill our children. She premeditated and meticulously planned the slaughter and carried it out in cold blood.

---

* "When peace comes we will perhaps in time be able to forgive the Arabs for killing our sons, but it will be harder for us to forgive them for having forced us to kill their sons." Meir, *A Land of Our Own*, 242.

MEIN KAMPF IN THE PLAYROOM 117

WHEN THE ZIONISTS BURNED OUR PEOPLE ALIVE IN THEIR TENTS in Rafah—a sentence I thought I would never write—the massacre was only interrupted by commercial breaks.* Their choir sang the same old tune, straight out of the playbook. At first they denied it, then they said it was a misfired rocket, then they said it was a precision attack on a military leader (who was hiding among civilians), then they said the number of martyrs was fabricated, then they said it was a tragic mistake.

As the screaming of the eyewitnesses grew louder, many of us debated what happened and worked hard to "debunk" Israeli claims. This distraction has always been the goal. Take an example I have already mentioned, Orwa Sheikh Ali, whose face was branded with the Star of David by Israeli police officers. The police claimed the marks were caused by an officer's shoe. Journalists, the stenographers they are, quickly amplified that official message. And, unfortunately, many of us took the bait and began to argue that shoelaces don't carve geometric signs onto skin, as if that is not already ridiculously obvious, as if the act of a settler policeman stomping on the face of a Palestinian is not itself outrageous. But the point is to confuse: the conversation shifted from being about the brutalized Palestinian young man to something completely irrelevant.

And the same playbook was used when an Israeli sniper shot and killed Shireen Abu Akleh, when Palestinian gunmen

---

* On May 26, 2024, the Israeli occupation forces targeted and bombed the "Kuwaiti Peace" displacement camp in the Tel al-Sultan refugee camp, Rafah, killing at least 50 people and injuring at least 249 people.

118   PERFECT VICTIMS

were accused of shooting her.[6] The same playbook was used when the Israeli regime bombed Al-Ahli Hospital, which was claimed to be destroyed in friendly fire.* The objective was not to prove that the IOF did not indeed bomb the hospital, but to create a frustrating, confusing public debate. "They kill the victim then march in his funeral."† Why do we indulge them? It is as though we have internalized their lines (*There are no innocents in Gaza. Palestinians are terrorists.*) and we are working to disprove it not only to our enemies and allies but even to ourselves.

So I return to the previous question: Is there room for side conversations in the presence of burning flesh? I am not suggesting we atrophy the muscle that powers our refutation reflex. Nor am I naively assuming that our movement can afford to not accommodate people's political journeys. Certainly, propaganda must be debunked. Certainly, we need to meet people where they are in order to move them. In these last few pages, I did not simply dismiss Zionist propaganda as if it were universally recognized as fables and fabrications. I did not immediately toss out Herzog's claims about *Mein Kampf.* Even though I know his allegations are deliberately deceptive, I still laid out for the reader the multitude of scenarios that might explain the book's presence in the room. I reminded the reader of how easy it is

---

* Mainstream news reports, even those that had reported on the bombing, backtracked and claimed "friendly fire," including the *New York Times.* See Kingsley and Boxerman, "Hamas Fails."

† Arab proverb. (يقتل القتيل ويمشي بجنازته)

MEIN KAMPF IN THE PLAYROOM 119

to obtain a copy, even in Israeli libraries, and that it could have been planted there by the soldiers themselves.

The idea is to "debunk" with dignity, always while naming the elephant in the room: propaganda. My mission is not to clear my name from false accusations; rather it is to unmask the deceit and duplicity of my accusers. Otherwise, logic in the face of illogic is short-sighted, because it unwittingly legitimizes insidiousness, it dignifies it with a response. If I say *Free Palestine* and someone hears *Holocaust*, that is at best apophenia, and at worst their own deliberate distortion, a deflection from the urgent and the tangible—the literal burning flesh of our people.

The morning I sat down to write this, a nurse and journalist named Yousef Mema published photos of the decomposing corpses of Palestinians murdered in the north of Gaza—a skull, a rib cage, and bones in the feet protruding through jeans. They had been exposed to the harsh elements for eighty days, he explained, because heavy Israeli bombardment and ground incursions had "prevented paramedics from reaching the martyrs." And all of this while young Palestinians in the US were being gunned down or stabbed by white supremacists.* Meanwhile, on another planet,

---

* Wadea al-Fayoume was a six-year-old Palestinian American boy living in Plainfield Township, Illinois. On October 14, 2023, he was stabbed twenty-six times by his white landlord in an anti-Palestinian hate crime. Hisham Awartani, Kinnan Abdalhamid, and Tahseen Ali Ahmad are three university students who were shot by a white man in Burlington, Vermont, on November 25, 2023. Zacharia Doar, a young Palestinian American father, was stabbed by a white man in Austin, Texas, on February 8, 2024. In a text read at a campus vigil and shared by the Palestinian Youth Movement, Hisham Awartani writes, "This

120   PERFECT VICTIMS

Zionist college students were busy decrying the threat posed by pro-Palestinian demonstrations on campus, then testifying about this threat in front of Congress. At first, I thought they were shedding crocodile tears. I thought they were feigning fear. But it cannot only be performance: despite the nukes and the promised homeland, their fear is so visceral it can conjure the Gestapo in the halls of the Ivy League.[7]

hideous crime did not happen in a vacuum. . . . I am but one casualty in this much wider conflict. Had I been shot in the West Bank, where I grew up, the medical services that saved my life here would likely have been withheld by the Israeli army."

MEIN KAMPF IN THE PLAYROOM 121

TO BE PALESTINIAN TODAY is to feel like you are caught in a fever dream—trapped in someone else's hallucination. It is to be interrogated about the hidden insidiousness of our chants while Israeli politicians boast about ethnically cleansing Gaza in newspapers and interviews. It is to be shouted over, silenced, by people who claim to fear for their lives from the safety of apartments that have never been blistered by white phosphorus, that have endured nothing fiercer than a US winter, while people in another corner of the planet dig for loved ones buried in the wreck of flattened buildings. Conversations about Palestine in the West are steered by abstractions, about the meaning of Zionism, about the threat level of words, about a logistically impossible yet impossibly imminent genocide of the Jewish people.*

Such details are not minor. In situating the Holocaust outside of history, in placing it not just in the past but in an eternal future, Zionism today has created a status quo in which the possibility of a second holocaust is given primacy over a holocaust happening in the present. I am certain some readers will find those previous lines uncomfortable or even incendiary, but that is precisely the point: language comparing Zionists to Nazis is scrutinized—even penalized—more than the government policies and military actions that beg for the analogy to be made. As long as this status quo persists,

---

* When I first published this passage, I was asked to clarify in writing that I am not a Holocaust denier, so I wrote "Apparently, I am supposed to clarify that I do believe the Holocaust happened." El-Kurd, "What Does It Mean."

as long as Palestinians are subjected to colonial violence and erasure, we certainly can and should refuse indignity as a state of being, refuse to shrink ourselves and our aspirations, refuse to be silenced or shouted over, and refuse to assuage the hallucinations of our colonizers.[8]

The idea is to spit out the bait and spit at the accusation. To demystify and reject what it is they demand of us: perfect victimhood and perfect surrender. The affective and kinesic performance with which we respond to such aspersions is often more resounding and gripping than the usual memorized statistics and pleas. By spelling out the pernicious subtext of a particular argument (or to simply reveal it through ridicule, dismissal, or repudiation), one disarms said argument, loosening the psychological grip it has on the listeners' minds. Otherwise, and as I have said before, cowering before a charge will often bring us closer to it, especially when our accusers hold their accusations to be self-evident.

How many people have we seen scrambling to write apologies and clarifications over accusations of anti-Palestinian racism or Islamophobia? Do those who interrupt our path to freedom with red herrings ever wonder about our well-being? If, in fact, "Hamas sent a seven-year-old girl wearing a Minnie Mouse sweatsuit right up to the [Israeli military barrier],"[9] how does that absolve the sniper who pulled the trigger? Isn't "she was asking for it" a pervert's argument? And if, indeed, there were tunnels and bunkers under Al-Shifa Hospital, how does that justify shelling it and killing those sheltering inside the building? If anything, what they call human shields are families who, even in death, will refuse separation, families who refuse to die anywhere but in each other's embrace.

▼

7.   *miraculous epiphanies*

If I die thirsty, may the rain never fall!
—Abu Firas al-Hamdani,
sung by Umm Kulthum*

A STONE'S THROW——**IT WAS A SCANDAL.** He threw what he later called "a pebble" at an Israeli guardhouse. Or watchtower (sources disagree).† Edward Said, the Palestinian intellectual, a giant of the academy, had engaged in actions that academics can only analyze, not partake in, during a visit to the South of Lebanon in July 2000. Outrage spread in the Ivy League and beyond. To call his actions "horseplay" was an understatement—there were not enough pearls to clutch.

Said's visit to the border came nearly forty days after Hezbollah had defeated the Israeli military and ejected them from Lebanese soil, ending twenty-two years of occupation and inspiring

---

* "Araka Asiya al-Dam,'" written around 960 AD. Umm Kulthum sang three different iterations of the poem, with the help of three composers. The most famous iteration was performed in 1964 and composed by Riadh al-Sunbati.
"إذا مِتّ ظَمْآناً فَلا نَزَل القَطْرُ!"
† Guarding what? Watching whom?

126   PERFECT VICTIMS

celebrations across the region. The academic, sixty-four years old
at the time, however, was "a little too portly, a little too distinguished to be hurling stones in the direction of Israeli soldiers,"
according to the *Washington Post*. Had the celebrated Columbia University professor "joined the ranks of Palestinian stone
throwers"? The question was not rhetorical; the *Post* answered in
the next sentence: "Apparently so."[1]

A week after that revelation, the *Columbia Daily Spectator*
featured on its front page a photograph of him hurling what
I hope was not a pebble but indeed a stone, with the headline "Edward Said Accused of Stoning in South Lebanon."[2]
Stoning. I assume such a word was chosen for its evocative,
Islamophobic connotations.* That it was hurled against the son
of Anglican Christian Arabs makes that choice especially racist. Yet reading that headline two decades later, one is almost
impressed by the craftsmanship of subtly writing racism into
double entendres, especially considering that today's headlines
know only to brashly pull the wool over our eyes. Take, for
example, the *Post*'s choice words in 2024 on the Israeli killing
of Palestinian children in a Gaza hospital: "Four Fragile Lives
Found Ended . . ."[3]

Those articles about Said were damning, but apparently not
damning enough. Two months later, some of Said's colleagues
responded in the *Daily Spectator*:

---

* Stoning, *rajm*, was never mentioned in the Quran. Only lashings, sooo . . .

> The opening sentence [of the *Washington Post* article] disturbs us, as it appears to imply that the act of hurling stones across an international border at unknown civilians and soldiers of a neighboring country would be acceptable or at least understandable if undertaken by ordinary younger, less portly or distinguished individuals. . . . Abhorrent and primitive as his gratuitous act of random violence [was] . . . it was all the more disturbing . . . having been committed by a colleague privileged to have been educated in the finest of private institutions worldwide.[4]

I do not know what is funnier: calling a maniacal settler-colonial entity a "neighboring country" or claiming that it is "gratuitous" and "primitive" to hurl stones at the settler colony. Yet neither is as comical as the fact that history's worst "gratuitous act[s] of random violence" have predominatly been carried out by people who trained at "the finest of private institutions."

Next it was not a colleague but one of Said's former students who had some moralizing words for him, all the way from Bet El, an Israeli colony in the occupied West Bank built in 1977 atop lands that belong to the villages of Beitin and Dura al-Qari'. The settlers of Bet El have for years enjoyed millions of dollars in tax-exempt donations from Jewish American charities like American Friends of Beit El* and benefactors such

---

* Other prominent US 501(c)(3)s dedicated to settlement expansion include the Irving Moskowitz Foundation, American Friends of Ateret Cohanim,

128   PERFECT VICTIMS

as Jared Kushner and David Friedman, whom Donald Trump would later appoint to prominent roles in his administration.[5]

"As I sipped my coffee," Said's settler student reported, "a picture of my old professor jumped out at me from my local Israeli newspaper."[6] I wonder on which of our stolen acres did the settler student experience such profound trauma. "There he was . . . throwing rocks over the fence at Jews in uniform who he knew would not respond."[7] First Obama, then this guy.[8] It seems as though Said was cursed with terrible students. How does one unironically describe none other than *Israeli soldiers* as innocuous "Jews in uniform who . . . would not respond"?

What delirium. This smug settler essay was penned thirteen years after Yitzhak Rabin, the West's beloved "Soldier of Peace," instructed the Israeli military to break the arms and legs of hundreds of stone throwers and peaceful protesters alike during the First Intifada, in what was dubbed Rabin's Break the Bones policy. What myopia. Just weeks after it was published, Israeli snipers targeted the eyes of the Second Intifada's rock-hurling children with rubber-coated steel bullets. Seventeen years later, in the 2018 Great March of Return, a new generation of Israeli snipers created a demographic of amputees in the besieged Gaza Strip as they shot-to-maim protesters who dared march toward their stolen hometowns. Too many events in Palestinian history have shown those Jews—and Druze and Muslims—in Israeli uniform to be

and the Central Fund of Israel, to name a few. See Shamas, "Tax Breaks for Colonization?"

MIRACULOUS EPIPHANIES 129

trigger-happy, if not outright genocidal. The specter of their nuclear arsenal looms over us. Their warplanes target our loved ones and burn them alive. *But Said's stone!* "What if [it] hit someone* on the other side?"[9]

* I wish it had.

IN THE FOLLOWING MONTHS, THE "SIGMUND FREUD SOCIETY" in Vienna canceled a lecture that Said was scheduled to give. The *New York Times* reported the cancellation in a story headlined "A Stone's Throw Is a Freudian Slip." The then-president of the Viennese organization told the paper that a lot of its members "can't accept that we have invited an engaged Palestinian who also throws stones against Israeli soldiers." From his perspective, Said was quoted arguing that his actions were a mere "symbolic gesture of joy" that the Israeli invasion of Lebanon had ended. "There was nobody there," he said. "The guardhouse was at least half a mile away."[10] That the academic felt it necessary to explain his "gratuitous" behavior, of course, cannot be separated from the hostility that colors the experiences of Palestinian scholars in the West. Yet the emphasis that the stone was in fact a "pebble" sticks out.

Perhaps it is through the previous quote, "There was nobody there," that one can understand Said's word choice. "Pebble" was possibly used in an attempt to illustrate the asymmetrical nature of the violent acts committed in this so-called conflict and the asymmetry of "the conflict" itself. Rocks versus tanks, David versus Goliath, and so on. Perhaps the word, then, was meant to highlight the trivial impact of stone throwing on the Israeli military and security apparatus, centering instead the metaphorical value of his act, be it "joy," defiance, or "solidarity with those Palestinians who were hurling stones at tanks and facing machine guns and bombing raids of the [IOF]."[11]

Another possibility was that Said felt an urge to clarify his principles. He was "very much against military occupation of

MIRACULOUS EPIPHANIES

131

any kind, whether by Israel of Arab countries, Iraq of Kuwait or whatever," he said. In a more cynical reading, one might interpret Said's remarks as an impulse to protect his positionality in the world, haplessly trying to control the damage. He threw *a pebble*, and in that discursive distinction he hoped to distance himself from the stone throwers and the tire burners, the *mekhablim,* and from violence altogether. He was, after all, a man of peace. "I have many Israeli friends. I've lectured in Israel and I continue to have contacts there," he said in a statement. "It's not hatred for Israel."[12]

I suspect that this explanation did nothing to assuage people's fury. Disclaimers of this sort often further implicate us in that of which we are accused, blowing smoke where there is no fire. In many people's eyes, the "portly" and "distinguished" intellectual, who "had been educated in the finest of private institutions," was no longer speaking the language of those who once embraced him in those institutions. "While it is not materially the same as blowing oneself up in a bus or cafe, the argument went, it is only steps removed, a kind of gateway activity."[13]

---

* *Mekhablim* (sing.: *mekhabel*) is a racial slur against Arabs. This uniquely Israeli word, often translated to "terrorist" though the closest equivalent is "saboteur," is used to refer to those who fall in the category of the condemned, i.e., Palestinians en masse, the Lebanese, Arabs, those deemed killable by the Israeli government, media, and military. For example, Palestinians arrested by the Israeli police are described as "mekhablim," no matter the circumstances of the arrest. Israeli media often use it to refer to entire Palestinian and Arab villages and cities, not just individuals, and to all Palestinian prisoners, regardless of the nature of the allegations leveled against them.

Escaping the genre of terrorism seems to be an impossible task, even for the most upwardly mobile and palatable of Palestinians. Said could no longer speak—he joined the ranks of "terrorists" and lost the angel he had so skillfully carved out of marble.

MIRACULOUS EPIPHANIES

WHO SPEAKS FOR PALESTINIANS? Who retains that right despite decades of demonization, delegitimization, and racial discrimination? Who can escape the genre of terrorism? If the most debonair and worldly among us cannot be trusted with a pebble, how could the unrefined be trusted with a microphone?

I have very little in common with Edward Said (beyond the Anti-Defamation League's* condemnation, which I consider a badge of honor). I am the product of a humble home and humble institutions, and, while poverty remains a material disadvantage across history, its social connotations, especially in the academy, have shifted. One could say that a humble background during his time was "déclassé" and is today cited heavily in college application essays as an admirable asset. I am also the child of astonishing absurdity. I grew up in half of my home, and the other half was stolen by Jewish settlers from Long Island, whose colonial endeavors, much like the settlers in Bet El, are also financed by tax-exempt American charities. I learned from

---

* Founded in 1913, the Anti-Defamation League (ADL), affectionately known as the "Apartheid Defense League," is a self-proclaimed "leading anti-hate organization in the world." The "civil rights" organization has historically spied on progressive movements, supported racist and militarized policing, smeared Black and Muslim activists, suppressed Palestinian rights, defamed critics of colonialism as antisemites, and allied itself with bigots. In August 2020, a coalition of progressive organizations launched the "Drop the ADL" campaign, arguing that "the ADL is not an ally" in social justice work. Notable signatories included the Democratic Socialists of America, Movement for Black Lives, Jewish Voice for Peace, Center for Constitutional Rights, and Council on American–Islamic Relations.

a young age to become a docent of dispossession, to synthesize and articulate those absurdities in broken English to the foreign diplomats and journalists who would sit in our "solidarity tent," drinking our tea and "witnessing" our catastrophe. It is these circumstances and articulations that have allowed me what merit and upward mobility allowed Said: the permission to narrate.

My tragedy, so to speak, and my willingness (and capacity)* to speak about it, has placed me in a unique position. On the one hand, I am a journalist, a writer. I occasionally get invited onto CNN—well, once; I never seem to get invited onto the same channel twice. On the other, I am a victim of forced displacement, a very public one to be precise, and this displacement has invited international attention. Why have I been given the mic? Is it because of the American accent I have rehearsed for years? Is it because I am easy on the eyes? Perhaps I have been given the mic to fill a perfunctory quota, to convey a semblance of fairness and even-handedness in the global conversation from which we are mostly erased. Sometimes, I cannot help but think that I and others in my shoes are atop podiums and in front of cameras merely as tokens rather than experts, simply there to entertain. Or have I been defanged?

---

* Not everybody can play the role of the advocate—especially not while they're grieving or struggling to keep food on the table. Nor does everybody desire to exhibit the wounds that have yet to heal in front of foreign diplomats and journalists eager to refute them.

MIRACULOUS EPIPHANIES 135

Today, I have found my answers. At eleven-years-old, when I was selected as the protagonist of a documentary about my neighborhood, Sheikh Jarrah, I had a very different answer to this question. I believed I was asked to speak because I was special.

136   PERFECT VICTIMS

What will you give birth to now?
A child . . . or a crime?

—Amal Dunqul[14]

CHILDREN ATOP THE PODIUM—**ON JERUSALEM'S JAFFA STREET,** fourteen years ago, I distinctly remember searching for nonprescription glasses to make myself look smart. It was just days before I was set to fly to the United States and Belgium, where I would address the US Congress and the European Parliament about forced expulsions (what the media called "evictions") in my neighborhood, Sheikh Jarrah. On the podium, wearing my fake glasses, I delivered the talking points that I had memorized, not knowing that I was the talking point. I do not recall much, except for the coldness of those rooms, some frowns, and some applause here and there. *Wow, they think I'm so mature and wise,* I thought.

A decade later, our street was back in the spotlight. We were campaigning once more alongside hundreds of my neighbors to save our homes from ethnic cleansing. What started as one neighborhood's rallying cry against dispossession translated into a unity uprising that situated the Palestinian cause at the center of the international news cycle. And so the politicians began to flock. I was contacted on behalf of the offices

*   "ماذا تلدين الآن؟
طفلًا . . .
أم جريمة؟"

of various American senators and congresspeople, including Chuck Schumer.

They were keen on speaking with Palestinians about what they always refer to as "the situation" in Jerusalem—a Jerusalem I call occupied and a Jerusalem they split and name "East Jerusalem"—though they did not want to talk to just *any* Palestinian. I was asked—this is a direct quote—whether I can "provide [them] with a Palestinian child who will present their dream of what peace means." To translate this request: the only Palestinian they are willing to let sit at their table is a child.[15] The only Palestinian deemed safe enough is a Palestinian whose fangs are yet to be sharpened. Otherwise the optics would offend their constituents and threaten their electoral chances. I understand the value of childhood because I have minted, or was swayed to mint, my status as a child into currency.

Western audiences, and increasingly audiences in Arab states that have normalized relations with the Zionist entity, much like their politicians, are not willing to engage adult Palestinians, let alone enraged adult Palestinians or scornful ones. In response, our political disenfranchisement and racial subjugation are then communicated through, and increasingly dependent on, a paradigm of "innocence," which turns our "analyses" into "accounts." Decontextualized, neutralized, and hyper-individualistic "accounts." In such a paradigm, not only do we have to exhibit the overt harm inflicted upon our children, we must also enunciate the overt harmlessness that defines and confines them. We practice a politics of appeal, transforming our children into persuasive talking points, hoping they will pull at the heartstrings of the heartless.

138   PERFECT VICTIMS

"**DEAR PRESIDENT OBAMA, I AM 14 . . .**"[16] These were the first words in an open letter I was asked to write to Obama in 2013. (I do not usually try to contact war criminals, but when I do, I make sure that, at the very least, they are recipients of the Nobel Peace Prize.) When Barack Hussein Obama first came to power, people had hope, for obvious reasons. My neighbor found hope in the president's middle name. He would insist that Obama was secretly Muslim, thus secretly anti-Zionist. "No, ma'am," I said, in the words of John McCain responding to someone asking if Obama was Arab, "No, ma'am. He's a decent family man citizen."*

I had not thought of my letter in eleven years, but it came to mind when I began writing this chapter. Initially, I thought it would serve as a compelling example of how children are ideal blank canvases for NGOs and political activists. Children are apolitical and impressionable; they will repeat after you. But as I reread it a decade later, one line jolted me into a deep, forgotten memory. "Mr. President, we want our houses back. *And our pre-1948 land*."[17] I immediately recalled myself on that day, leaning against the doorway of our living room, cradling the landline to my ear, listening to two *Guardian* editors with posh accents, arguing with them using my limited English. I insisted on making clear in the letter that I wanted the return of not only the cities occupied in 1967 but all of our stolen land, even the land that had been recognized by international borders as legitimate

---

* McCain was responding to an audience member at a 2008 town hall in Lakeville, Minnesota.

MIRACULOUS EPIPHANIES

parts of the colony. To the editors, that was a problematic line to keep in the text. It was a demand for total decolonization.

Still, I gave them an ultimatum, as a blossoming teenager would, and they published the draft without mutilating it. "If I had one wish," the letter concludes, "I would get everyone's rights back. From a little ball they stole from a boy in the street to a big farm they stole from a grandfather." (Obama responded to me three years later, albeit subliminally, by offering the Israeli regime $38 billion in military funding in what was, at the time, the largest aid package of its kind in US history.)

That memory unraveled much of what I had come to accept about child advocates, and children in general. How does one define childhood? What do children have to say about the world around them? My little sister, Maha, had just turned seven years old when a settler ran over and killed five-year-old Enas Khalil* with his car. I often wondered whether Maha thought of Enas as she crossed the street on her way to school. Does a seven-year-old in Jerusalem or the South of Lebanon develop in similar ways to a seven-year-old New Yorker? Are seven-year-olds in Tribeca and the South Bronx the same? What does a boy selling gum at the Qalandiya military checkpoint have in common with a boy attending boarding school in Switzerland? What can a girl in Tel Aviv say to a girl from Tulkarem?

---

* Enas Khalil (2009–2014) was a Palestinian girl from the village of Sinjil, north of Ramallah. On October 19, 2014, Enas was walking home with her friend Tulin Asfour when a settler ran them over with his car, killing Enas and severely wounding Tulin.

IN WHAT REALMS DO CHILDREN ENCOUNTER ONE ANOTHER? I was two and a half years old when I first encountered Muhammad al-Durrah on a television screen, crouching behind his father. He taught me, in spite of himself, the word "martyr."* Fifteen years later, I encountered Ahmad Manasra on my cell phone. He had also been run over by a car, in a settlement fifteen minutes from my school. Ahmad's head was bleeding, and his legs twisted behind him as the crowd around him shouted in Hebrew: *Die, son of a bitch!*

And on that exact same day, Marah Bakir† was sixteen and I was seventeen. We were both on our respective ways home. Our paths crossed as I approached Sheikh Jarrah. All the passengers on the bus turned to the left. I looked outside the window and saw Marah laying in a pool of her blood. The police had fired at her and accused her of the usual. I learned her name in the hours

---

* Muhammad al-Durrah (1988–2000) was a twelve-year-old Palestinian boy who was killed by the Israeli occupation forces in the Gaza Strip at the beginning of the Second Intifada. He was shot on September 30, 2000, as he crouched behind his father, Jamal, in a murder that was broadcast live worldwide. On October 15, 2023, Jamal al-Durrah's brothers were killed in an Israeli airstrike on the Gaza Strip, and on January 18, 2024, twenty-three years after killing Muhammad, the IOF killed his brother, Ahmad, in Bureij camp in Gaza.

† Marah Bakir is a Palestinian former political prisoner from Beit Hanina, occupied Jerusalem. On October 12, 2015, Bakir was shot by Israeli occupation forces and accused of stabbing an Israeli police officer in Sheikh Jarrah, Jerusalem. She was sentenced to eight and a half years in prison at sixteen years old. Bakir was one the prisoners released on November 24, 2023, in a prisoner exchange deal.

MIRACULOUS EPIPHANIES

that followed.* On Marah's sixth year in prison, my neighbor and little sister's classmate Nufooz Hammad† would be apprehended from her school by police. They accused her of the usual. Had Nufooz heard of Marah before or was she only introduced to her in prison?‡

What do children make of incarceration? Walid Daqqa§ wrote that he had, for a long time, avoided using the term "prison" with his daughter Milad when talking about where he resided, where he was held hostage.[18] Milad, who must have been two or three years old at the time, "came to understand what a

---

* Ahmad Manasra is a Palestinian political prisoner from Beit Hanina, occupied Jerusalem. He was arrested in 2015 at thirteen years old, accused of partaking in a stabbing against settlers in Pisgat Ze'ev, an Israeli settlement in occupied Jerusalem. He was sentenced to nine and a half years in Israeli prison and has been in solitary detention since November 2021. His case has received international coverage for the physical and psychological torture imposed upon him by the Zionist state.

† Nufooz Hammad is a former political prisoner from Sheikh Jarrah. In 2021, at fourteen years old, she was accused of attempting to stab one of the settlers who lived across the street in the Al-Ghawi family home, which had been forcibly taken by a government-backed settler organization in 2008. She was sentenced to twelve years in Israeli prison. She was the youngest Palestinian female prisoner in Israeli custody. She was also released alongside Marah Bakir in the prisoner exchange deal.

‡ Both Nufooz and Marah were among the 117 Palestinian women and child detainees released in a prisoner exchange deal between the settler state and Hamas in late November 2023.

§ Walid Daqqa (1961–2023) is the longest-serving Palestinian political prisoner in Israeli jails. He is a writer, novelist, and philosopher. In 2019, he smuggled sperm out of an Israeli prison to give life to his only daughter, Milad, only one year after he wrote a young adult novel about a teenage boy conceived in the same way, titled *The Oil's Secret Tale*.

prison is long before she learned the meaning of the word. To her it was a place without a door." What becomes of children swallowed into such a place?* "In the world of prison," Walid argued, "childhood is a burden." Children, "in the face of the cruelty of [prison] guards," become eager to abandon their vulnerability. He was writing about an encounter with a twelve-year-old child prisoner—what a phrase, "child prisoner"—who asked Daqqa for a cigarette.

> In normal circumstances, outside the walls of the prison, I would have said no. We don't want children to smoke. But in this environment, it struck me that the child wanted by this request to grow up quickly so that he could better confront the years of confinement that now loomed before him or perhaps recover from the violence of his arrest. By the act of smoking, he seemed to proclaim, "Behold me, an adult." So I handed the child a cigarette.[19]

The child prisoner, who was in the early days of his four-year sentence, did not want to smoke; he wanted the act of smoking to harden him in the eyes of his jailers. "He wanted to become a man quickly."[20] What can one say to boys who become men in a hurry? Where do those who resemble Rami Hamdan, Tamir Rice, and Cassius Turvey end up in a world that hunts them?

---

* There were 240 Palestinian children in Israeli prisons in June 2024. See Zhang, "Israel Is Currently Imprisoning."

MIRACULOUS EPIPHANIES 143

Where do they flee? "To church"? "To other ghettos"?* Or do they go on to "whiskey or the needle"?[21] Boys, in such a world, are men, and girls are men, and the women are men too.[22] Not only men but fighters, who all seem, through a sniper's world-view, to be plotting the sniper's demise.

> The [prison] guard shouted at [the child prisoner] to drop the cigarette and then muttered to himself in Hebrew, bemoaning the sight of a child smoking. Nevertheless he proceeded with the handcuffing, remaining unmoved by the sight of those small hands in handcuffs. Because the child's wrists were too small, however, he struggled several times to secure the handcuffs, and finally decided to use them to chain the boy's legs.[23]

Daqqa saw a son in the twelve-year-old, a fearful, fragile son. He wanted to parent him, to embrace him, and to weep over his injustice, but he heeded the boy's wishes. "I hid my feelings," he explained. Do children have agency? Is that why the Black Panther Party insisted on providing them a political education?[24] Is that why Daqqa and Kanafani addressed them directly in *Hikayat Sir al-Zait* and *al-Qindeel al-Sahir*?[25] The child prisoner Daqqa encountered walked a tightrope in his attempt to prove

---

* "When I was ten, and didn't look, certainly, any older," James Baldwin writes, "two policemen amused themselves with me by frisking me, making comic (and terrifying) speculations concerning my ancestry and probable sexual prowess, and, for good measure, leaving me flat on my back in one of Harlem's empty lots." Baldwin, "Letter from a Region in My Mind."

to himself and others that he was bigger than the dark chambers of prison. He wanted to achieve mobility for himself inside its walls. Jail is an odd place to find freedom, but one tends to look for it there anyway.* "I did not want to shatter the image of the man that he wanted now to become," Daqqa explained. "I walked over to him, so as to shake his hand as a comrade, and a rival, asking, *How are you, fighter?*"

Can little boys be fighters? We have seen them, in images on the internet, their sunburnt faces frowning and their small torsos weighed down by the straps of rifles. At twelve or so they "know by heart the names of the elders who took part in the last revolt," they dream of heroes "whose heroic death[s] still bring tears to their eyes."[26] We read about them in Bangladesh, illiterate and disguising themselves as tea shop workers, blowing up enemy detention camps, receiving awards they cannot read or pronounce.† Can children be heroes? We read about them in Jenin, driving on their bikes through explosives and debris to deliver food and medicine to the wounded and besieged in the

---

* "Jail is an odd place to find freedom, but that was the place I first found mine . . ." Newton, *Revolutionary Suicide*, 99.

† Shahidul Islam Lalu was a child guerrilla fighter in the Mukti Bahini, a Bangladeshi resistance group, during the 1971 Bangladesh Liberation War. At the age of twelve, he played a pivotal role in a strategic offensive by bombing and destroying two Pakistani bunkers in Gopalpur Upazila, Tangail, Bangladesh. For his bravery, he became the youngest recipient of the *Bir Protik*, a gallantry award granted by the Bangladeshi government. Lalu was born into a poor farming family from Gopalpur and was illiterate. Despite this recognition, after the war ended, he remained unaware that he had received the award. Amna Ali, in conversation.

refugee camp.* We hear them on the road to Jericho, their tired voices demanding we lower our car windows to buy their last box of tissues. We hear about them becoming the world's youngest journalists,† they describe it as a "responsibility . . . duty . . . an obligation" to probing adults overseas.‡ We hear them reporting about their stolen homes and slain siblings, about impending death, about resuscitation. Should they be heroes?

They address us but we do not address them back. We speak about them in third person, looking away when they chase us with their gaze. We think about them as an unfortunate problem in our peripheral vision. But they are a symptom of a rotten world, an indictment of the world we have created. Much like the prison guards "bemoaning the sight of a child smoking," we are sickened by the thought of child fighters. Who wants to see a sullen girl throw a Molotov cocktail? Nevertheless, we continue pushing them to a suffocating edge. Like the prison guards, we remain "unmoved by the sight of those small hands in handcuffs."

---

* In 2024, during one of the largest raids on Jenin. See Jarrar interview for Al Jazeera.

† In 2016, then ten-year-old Janna Jihad was described as "the youngest journalist in Palestine." Then, in 2023, "proudly sporting a press vest and helmet, interviewing adults and children alike," nine-year-old Lama Jamous became "internationally known for her reporting on the ongoing genocide in Gaza." See Sarkar, "Janna Jihad"; and *New York War Crimes*, "Lama Jamous' Reporting."

‡ "The Future of Gaza."

I TOO AM AGAINST A CHILD——ANY CHILD——BEARING A GRENADE.[27] But the world needs to contend with the fact that childhood, in the context of the oppressed, is deformed beyond recognition, not because of cultural regression as the colonists love to argue, or because "we teach our children to hate," but because of the ceaseless colonial degradation of children and their families in our world.

People will make the argument that merit and hard work can triumph over chance and circumstance. But can one truly escape their class? "One [does] not have to be very bright," James Baldwin argued, "to realize how little one could do to change one's situation; one did not have to be abnormally sensitive to be worn down to a cutting edge by the incessant and gratuitous humiliation and danger encountered" by living alongside one's dehumanizers.* There have been many claims about links between early intervention and child development. That if Palestinian children were provided with the educational and psychological support they desperately need, they could better confront the trauma and long-lasting effects of military occupation.[28] But the brutal reality of colonial violence, as it manifests not only in constant exposure to checkpoints, raids, and settler and military violence but also in the relentless attacks on their personhood, confirms that no amount of support, outside of abolishing colonial rule in Palestine, can shield children from the deep and last-

---

* In "Letter from a Region in My Mind," Baldwin was referring to the friends he had grown up with in Harlem.

MIRACULOUS EPIPHANIES 147

ing scars left by the erosion of their daily lives. *Arna's Children* comes to mind.*

At the beginning of the film, several Palestinian boys and girls, all younger than eight years old, are receiving art therapy at a theater in Jenin, sometime in the early 1990s.† One of the boys is hopping around, imitating a cat. "This is Nidal," the narrator says, "he is the youngest one in the group. In six years' time, during the Al-Aqsa Intifada, Nidal will join the Islamic Jihad movement and will be killed during the fighting against the Israeli army." Despite the crayons, the workshops, and the best intentions, despite the "early intervention," the brutality of the colonizer, which has devastated their communities and sense of safety, pushed those children, most of them at least, toward armed struggle. Several of them would fight against the Israeli occupation forces in the Second Intifada or play key roles in the 2002 Battle of Jenin.

---

* *Arna's Children* is a documentary chronicling the lives of Palestinian children in the Jenin refugee camp and their involvement in a local theater group started by Arna Mer-Khamis. Some of these children grew to become Palestinian resistance fighters. The documentary intersperses their childhood in the theater with them taking up arms as adults, and eventually their martyrdom.

† Arna Mer-Khamis (1929–1995) was a Jewish teacher and activist born in the settlement of Rosh Pinna, Upper Galilee, occupied Palestine. She was the founder of Care and Learning, an art therapy organization that inspired the Jenin Freedom Theater, cofounded by her son Juliano in the Jenin refugee camp in 2006. She won the Right Livelihood Award in 1993 for her "passionate commitment to the defense and education of the children of Palestine."

148   PERFECT VICTIMS

Another boy, in a striped shirt, playfully barks at Nidal. "This is his brother Yussef. Yussef is the joker in the group," the narrator continues. "In five years' time, in October 2001, Yussef and his friend . . . will commit a suicide attack in Israel."[29]

> And this is Ashraf. Ashraf is Yussef's best friend. We used to call Ashraf "shorty with the big smile." During the Al-Aqsa Intifada, Ashraf will lead the group of fighters in the Battle of Jenin. I met Ashraf for the first time when he was nine years old, in the ruins of his house. His house was destroyed when the house next door was blown up by the Israeli army. This is where his friend Ala was living. . . . In eight years' time, Ala will become the leader of Al-Aqsa Brigade in Jenin.

One of the film's protagonists is Zakaria Zubeidi, whose mother and brother were shot dead by the occupation forces during the Battle of Jenin. He is a former member of the Al-Aqsa Martyrs Brigade and one of Arna's children. In 2021, he, among five others, participated in the legendary prison break from the maximum-security Gilboa prison.[30] In an old interview of his that has resurfaced, Zubeidi tells the camera: "I want my son to be educated, to live a life better than the one I live. I would love for him to obtain scientific degrees, to become a doctor, a lawyer, an engineer; that is my dream. And I will work to achieve it, but the Israelis have to first allow my child to grow up."[31] His son Mohammed Zubeidi went on to join the resistance. On September 5, 2024, at just twenty-one years old, Mohammed, alongside four others, was killed by the

MIRACULOUS EPIPHANIES

149

Israeli military during an incursion in Tubas, in the occupied West Bank.[32]

The very moment that the Palestinian exits the womb, he is "unchilded"—flung away from childhood by a "machinery that exists everywhere and always" and treated as both a good-for-nothing nobody and a dangerous ticking bomb at once.[33] The Palestinian is unchilded the first time he talks to his uncle from behind glass or asks his aunt about the tin roofs or tries to decipher what has been erased from the street signs. Or when he embraces his father by a concrete cylinder, telling himself that the explosions he is hearing are just fireworks. Or when he plays soccer on the beach.* Somewhere along the line the Palestinian child will stumble across the phrase "legally killed child" used to describe his slain peers; a Yale professor will write a column in the *Atlantic* about how "it is possible to kill children legally."[34] And the sniper follows orders.

The Palestinian is unchilded the first time she passes the checkpoint on her way to school and feels the weight of a stranger's hand under her shirt, the first time she sits next to her classmate's empty desk, leaving her yet another rose. Or when she takes the bus home and looks outside the window to see another schoolgirl in a coagulating pool. She is exiled from childhood the first time she asks about the black ribbon on her mother's photograph or why the neighbors weep when they congratulate.

---

* On July 16, 2014, four boys aged between nine and fourteen—Ismail Bakr, Zakaria Bakr, Ahed Bakr, and Mohamed Bakr—were killed by Israeli naval fire while playing soccer on a beach in Gaza City.

The first time she skips rocks across a sea of camo green or douses a piece of cloth before stuffing it down a bottleneck, or when she feels the steel cocoon becoming a butterfly inside her knee.* The first time the Palestinian boy hears the banging of the gavel or feels the coldness of steel on his small wrists, he is forced into adulthood. He watches his reflection in a pool of spit; he finds gray in his hair. He grows under the moon of fluorescent lighting, coming of age in the interrogation room.

---

* Expanding bullets (or dum-dum bullets), more colloquially known as "butterfly bullets," are designed to expand or break apart on impact, tearing through tissue and bone and creating multiple wound channels. The fragmentation of the bullet causes severe internal injury, spreading throughout the body.

MIRACULOUS EPIPHANIES

MANY, IF NOT MOST, DIPLOMATIC AND CULTURAL APPEALS made in favor of the Palestinian plight exploit childhood to make a case for our humanity. Proponents of this tactic, whether malicious or well-meaning, rationalize it in all sorts of ways. To some, *It is one of the only viable political strategies in such a hostile political climate*, while to others, *It is not about politics; it is about universal values*. But none of those rationalizations attack the racism at the heart of this phenomenon. It is the dehumanization of Palestinians, one Nakba at a time, that has led us here: the demonization of our people, one Intifada at a time: the demonization of the Palestinian man, in particular, that has driven us to situate our humanity in childhood, a state that is supposedly divorced from politics.

But what many fail to consider is that even children are not spared the sniper's bloodlust. "Wait, you're saying children in Gaza are being shot by snipers?" a CBS News correspondent asks Dr. Mark Perlmutter, an orthopedic surgeon who has just returned from Gaza. "Definitively," he answers. "I have two children that I have photographs of that were shot so perfectly in the chest, I couldn't put my stethoscope over their heart more accurately."[35] And if children cannot escape Zionist fire, what makes us believe that somehow, by virtue of their age, they escape the dehumanization and racism of the Zionist apparatus that discredits our academics and demonizes our journalists? The sniper lurks not only atop our homes but in conference rooms and newsrooms, on university campuses and in hospital corridors.

In February 2023, the Chelsea and Westminster Hospital in London succumbed to pressure from the Zionist group UK

Lawyers for Israel (UKLFI) and took down a display of artworks by Palestinian schoolchildren. According to UKLFI, which was "delighted" by the outcome, the complaint to the hospital was made on behalf of a number of Jewish patients who, hilariously, infuriatingly, "said that they felt vulnerable and victimized by this display."[36] Salaried adults. Nothing evades the Zionist backlash: not the most docile of children's books nor painted ceramic plates created by children in Gaza; neither do the decorated academics, nor do I.

I am no longer a child, and childhood can no longer serve as the ethos of my argument. Like all Palestinian men, I am viewed through a fundamentally racist lens, not through my articulations or my character. Any campus I visit, I am welcomed by warmth, of course, but also by flyers, op-eds, and statements that seek to discredit me as a spokesperson on the Occupation despite my life as an occupied subject.* So if I can't always get the mic, who can? If Edward Said cannot get the mic, if our children cannot get the mic, who can? Who has the permission to narrate?

---

* When I first gave the Perfect Victims lecture at Princeton University, it was delivered in an auditorium surrounded by and packed with cops. There were multiple articles, statements, and flyers protesting this lecture before it even began.

Many books, particularly then . . . [I] could feel the address of the narrator over my shoulder talking to somebody else, talking to somebody white. I could tell because they were explaining things that they didn't have to explain if they were talking to me.

—Toni Morrison[37]

MIRACULOUS EPIPHANIES—**EVERY SO OFTEN, A ZIONIST COMES OUT AND SAYS IT.** Perhaps it is a politician boasting, "We are now rolling out the Gaza Nakba,"* or "Beirut must burn,"† or defending a soldier's right to rape Palestinian prisoners.‡ One does not need to dig deep to discover an abundance of genocidal, racist, and expansionist rhetoric from Israeli public figures and national institutions. It is enough to turn on Israeli television, translate random Hebrew social media posts, or read Zionist news outlets. Such statements are not always uttered with such insolence and hubris. Sometimes it is a prudent revelation or an accidental admission straight from the horse's mouth that affirms what we have said all along.

---

* Israeli agriculture minister and security cabinet member Avi Dichter to Channel 12, November 11, 2023.

† Former minister Yoaz Hendel, on Israel's Kan television, September 2024.

‡ When asked if it was legitimate "to insert a stick into a person's anus," Hanoch Milwidsky, a member of Knesset, responded, "If he is a [Hamas militant], everything is legitimate to do! Everything!" Cordall, "'Everything Is Legitimate.'"

PERFECT VICTIMS

Occasionally a liberal Zionist newspaper runs a headline confirming that "Israel is a settler-colonial state"[38] or prints an op-ed by a former attorney general who asserts, "We established an apartheid regime in the occupied territories."[39] Some former ministers have likewise warned, out of concern for their settler colony, that their policies are violent, despotic, and, most important, unsustainable.* The pages of the diaries and manifestos of Zionism's forefathers overflow with similar admissions. To show that Zionism weaponizes antisemitism, we cite Herzl,† who said, "The anti-Semites will become our most dependable friends, the anti-Semitic countries our allies."[40] To justify our resistance, we cite a self-aware Jabotinsky,‡ who wrote in Russian that Palestinians "look upon Palestine with the same instinctive love and true fervor that any Aztec looked upon his Mexico or any Sioux looked upon his prairie." That there is no precedent of "any colonization being carried on with the consent of the native population. . . . The native populations, civilized or uncivilized, have always stubbornly resisted the colonists."[41]

---

* "If the day comes when the two-state solution collapses, and we face a South African-style struggle for equal voting rights, then, as soon as that happens, the state of Israel is finished." Former prime minister Ehud Olmert in an interview with *Haaretz* in 2010.

† Born in Pest, Hungary, Theodor Herzl (1860–1904) was one of the most prominent pioneers of Zionism. He is known for authoring *Der Judenstaat* in 1896 and forming the World Zionist Organization in 1897, through which he promoted the colonization of Palestine.

‡ Vladimir Jabotinsky (1880–1940) cofounded the Irgun, the Zionist paramilitary responsible for the bombing of the King David Hotel in Jerusalem in 1946 and the Deir Yassin massacre in April 1948.

MIRACULOUS EPIPHANIES

Such revelations are occasionally propelled by a sense of moral urgency: an Auschwitz survivor will say, *Never again for anyone*; a young refusenik will publicly oppose occupation. Or it is moral superiority: a settler in Palestine will make a film about other, worse settlers, who laugh as they testify about Tantura, where they buried our ancestors in mass graves, a massacre we have narrated for decades, with visceral recollection, in our movies, in our novels and songs, in our oral histories. On other occasions, it is remorse that takes them to the confession booth: a soldier suffers a pang of conscience and decides to break his silence, after a long career of maiming children or hunting protesters for sport. He comes clean, under legal immunity, of course, about all the heinous acts he has committed in our towns and refugee camps. He cannot sleep, he has PTSD, so, naturally, he embarks on a speaking tour across universities, where he is met with applause and platitudes. He professes his sins in the confessional of a brightly lit stage, and the audience, unscathed, entertained, grants him a plenary indulgence. What courage.

We are obsessed with such soliloquies. In literature and in the media, in many activist and civil society circles, we are quick to quote these people: the Zionist pioneers, the foul-mouthed politicos, the soldiers who shoot and cry. We rush to invoke the belated miraculous epiphanies of Israeli human rights organizations, the epiphanies of former ministers who corroborate our aged allegations. But as much as people like to hear it "from the horse's mouth," that mouth is not always reliable. Israeli officials are proficient and highly trained in the art of pretenses. They are maestros of hypocrisies and half-truths. Prone to slipping up in a moment of televised fury, they are also capable of reading the room. Of justifying murder and theft in between the lines. Of worshiping war with dizzyingly robust language. And they have done so for decades. I have heard many speeches about peace and coexistence while tear gas bombs filled our kitchen with fumes.

Still, when Bezalel Smotrich* claims there is "no such thing as a Palestinian people," he is rebuffed—even the White House has something to say.[42] His negationist remarks are an affront to the international community, whereas the actual deracination of the Palestinian People is business as usual; that we are invisibilized through policy and procedure, that we are denied both our past and our future, is standard protocol. It is the articulation of the de facto, not the de facto itself, that triggers the diplomatic hiccup. What is it about words, *their words*, that carries so much?

I am native to Jerusalem, whether Jabotinsky admits it or not. And reading Herzl is no prerequisite to understanding that the Zionists have colonized Palestine. It is enough to look around at the ruins of countless depopulated villages, at the bulldozers and the freshly erected flags, to find the ubiquitous evidence of ethnic cleansing staring you in the face. I know that Zionists and antisemites are brothers in arms; I am reminded of it each time Netanyahu and John Hagee† embrace. I could tell you, in

---

* Sunburnt loser. Israeli Finance Minister and cofounder of Regavim, a settler organization that works to expand settlments in the West Bank and advocates for the demolition of Palestinian villages. He is a self-described "fascist homophobe." His family is from Ukraine.

† John Hagee is an American pastor and televangelist. He is the founder and chairman of the Christian Zionist organization Christians United for Israel.

MIRACULOUS EPIPHANIES

vivid detail, about my grandparents' Nakba and my own; just as the Lebanese could tell you about Sabra and Shatila, about the 1982 invasion, and the invasion being carried out as I write these words; just as the Egyptians could tell you about the War of Attrition in 1969, the 1970 bombing of Bahr al-Baqar primary school, just as the Iraqis could tell you about the Baghdad Bombings in the 1950s. I see their flames devouring our cities. I hear the long-ignored cries of our political prisoners, subjected to the most perverse kinds of violence, and I wait for the Israeli correspondent to "break" the story that Palestinians journalists have broken once, twice, so many times before. Why do we give the authority of narration to those who have murdered and displaced us when the scarcity of their guilt means honesty is unlikely? Why do we wait for those carrying the batons to confess when our bruised bodies tell the whole truth?

When we speak of these horrors, inherent to Zionist ideology, we are perceived at best as passionate and at worst, angry and hateful. But in reality, we are simply reliable narrators. I say we are reliable narrators not because we are Palestinians. It is not on an identitarian basis that we must claim the authority to narrate. Rather it is because history tells us that those who have oppressed, who have monopolized and institutionalized violence, will not tell the truth, let alone hold themselves

---

Hagee, who once said in a sermon that Hitler was sent from God to "hunt" "the Jews," is frequently invited by Zionist groups to speak at pro-Israel rallies. Despite having said, "Jews will suffer for eternity in hell," he is embraced by the likes of Netanyahu. Mathis-Lilley, "Critics Question."

accountable.[43] Meaning, for every attorney general who says, "Israel is an apartheid state," there are a dozen others who will argue that it is "the only democracy in the Middle East." For every refusenik, there is a European youth who will gleefully volunteer to serve in the occupation forces. For every Israeli Holocaust survivor who opposes the genocide in Gaza, there is another hugging his grandchild as the latter embarks on a killing spree in the starved, besieged concentration camp.

PALESTINIANS CAN ONLY SPEAK, OR BE SPOKEN FOR, through slick rhetorical devices, pandering, and favorable endorsements. Such practices have dominated Western institutions for decades, producing a muzzled, undignified discourse and keeping advocacy efforts on a tight leash. And in a mainstream hostile to Palestinians, one resorts to a formulaic approach to talking about Palestine. Writers and filmmakers, for instance, frequently begin their essays or documentaries by denouncing antisemitism. The savvier ones choose a subtler tactic: introducing the viewer to a Neturei Karta member donning a *shtreimel* and a keffiyeh or starting the reader's journey in Yad Vashem. The analysis in these projects is habitually sourced from liberal Israeli correspondents and Western commentators, and the history cited in them is penned by Israeli scholars. They confirm, corroborate, and verify, whereas we allege and claim. We provide the raw material from which they extract their authenticated reports.

I know this firsthand and experienced this almost every day when I would get home from school. Field workers and human rights researchers were constant guests in our house in Sheikh Jarrah, eating maqluba from our table every Friday, eager to see the images, often printed on poster boards, of soldiers assaulting my grandmother, of our tear-gassed neighbors, of my aunt on a stretcher. They were hungry to learn the psychological toll of living under military occupation, adamant to hear the stories of verbal abuse and sexual harassment we have endured from settlers. But as soon as I attempted to offer any analysis, it felt as though they stopped listening—the analysis was reserved for the

160   PERFECT VICTIMS

"real experts." Only they had the license to audit and interpret our trauma; only they had the license to frame and abstract.

This formula is pervasive across mediums—and depressingly easy to trace. It has become a habit of mine to read the works cited section of Palestine-related books before I read the actual books, including Palestinian-authored books, and the list of references is generally predictable: Ilan Pappé or Benny Morris, depending on one's political leanings, Ir Amim, Breaking the Silence, and Yesh Din, Amnesty International and Human Rights Watch, *Haaretz* and *+972*, the *Jerusalem Post* and the *Times of Israel*, and a smattering of Western media outlets. If we are lucky, the list will include one or two dead Palestinian academics. If anything, this blueprint makes for bad and boring literature.

There are, of course, consequential differences between a refusenik who has not shed blood and a repentant soldier soaked in it; ideological differences between Ilan Pappé and Benny Morris. I make no effort here to comment on the quality or usability of the interventions provided by the aforementioned names and organizations. I am interested in interrogating the drive toward this politics of appeal. The premise that Jews, Israelis, and Westerners are less biased or more truthful is entirely unfounded, for it presumes they have no skin in the game. And the itch to continually cite their institutions is, in debate terms, argumentum ad verrecundiam.

This persuasive technique is, in this case, fallacious because it does not appeal to their authority as human rights organizations, but to their authority as Jewish (or European or American) institutions, first and foremost. One popular television host asks: "Is B'Tselem, an acclaimed *Israeli* human rights organization *staffed by Jewish Israelis*, antisemitic for accusing Israel of creating an 'apartheid regime'? How about Yesh Din, another *Israeli* human rights organization *staffed by Jewish Israelis*?"[44] Here, the crime of apartheid, which manifests through systemic racial domination, takes a back seat. The debate becomes about pondering whether one can characterize the settler state in such terms without committing a crime that, in this day and age, is more brutal and ravaging than apartheid: prejudice against Jewish people. If such specious reasoning is "strategic," what does that reveal about our world?

One explanation could be that the author (or documentarian, or high schooler giving a presentation) recognizes there is a conscious or a subconscious prejudice preventing recipients from digesting Palestinian testimonies, that the author, in their own assessment, acknowledges their readers to be racist. Here, holding a mirror to one's audience proves to be a difficult choice, whereas coddling them is the more popular one. Yet the strategy of favoring non-Palestinian voices does little to bypass the reader's anti-Palestinian bias. Instead, it reifies that bias and the power structures that manufacture it, cementing the impression that Palestinian voices are suspicious or subpar.

The absence of Palestinian knowledge producers in such projects is not a testament to the inferiority of Palestinian knowledge production but an *indictment* of the erasure that lingers across industries—an erasure that refuses to engage with Palestinian historians like Aref al-Aref, Salman Abu Sitta, and Rosemarie Janet Said Zahlan, and dismisses organizations such as Al-Haq, Addameer, and Adalah. It reflects the racism that cites Israeli officials first, while only offering the podium to Palestinians who have survived tragedies of epic proportions, demanding they make concession after concession and disavowal after disavowal. A racism that expunges us from the bibliography.

When Palestinians finally arrive in these works, on the screen or on the page, we are represented as victims, not as protagonists or complex characters. We are not history makers; history stomps on our bodies. Our resistance is obscured, our lineages defaced. We offer our blood and bruises as evidence, reporting our calamities without commentary, to support the author's thesis. We become their objects—curated into context-free exhibitions, editorialized to wallow unintelligibly. "No legends, no explanations." These words were the UN's response to a request by Edward Said to hang photographs of Palestinians in the entrance hall of the 1983 International Conference on the Question of Palestine in Geneva. The UN, where Said was working as a consultant at the time, agreed to his idea, but on the condition that "no writing can be displayed with [the photographs]. No legends, no explanations."[45]

Perhaps another reason underlying our dependence on such rhetorical devices—be it decorated Western expertise or defanged Palestinian testimony—is simply that it is what sells. It was disorienting, albeit sobering, to realize that advocating for Palestine, like all things, is entrenched in and informed by capitalism, that there was a market for our suffering, something that, for many, may have already been self-evident. In this reality, not only are Palestinian cultural and national symbols commodified, but the Palestinian himself becomes a commodity, the audience, of course, the consumer. The market demands we manufacture a manicured version of the Palestinian, meant to serve one purpose before anything else: to entertain. To sustain itself, this industry of commercialized advocacy becomes depressingly reliant on a set of tried-and-true tropes, mythmaking, and sensationalized spectacles that satisfy in the consumer an almost lubricious craving.

Take the genre of Israelis and Palestinians making films together. The Palestinian filmmaker is chaperoned to the film festival, allowed on stage as their authoritative cosignatory's charismatic sidekick. No one—not the producer of the festival, not the columnist writing a review—seems to care about the *content* of the film, whether it is good or garbage. What matters most is that the film was *codirected*, a mode that satisfies a libidinal urge in the viewers. They eavesdrop on a forbidden conversation, a titillating reconciliation between the slayer and the slain. Discussions about the film, reviews, the way it is promoted, and our excited elevator pitches to one another all become masturbatory, reducing the film to the fact that it was a collaboration between an Israeli and a Palestinian, fulfilling the viewer's fantasy of a happy ending to an otherwise miserable story. We turn it into a fetish.

Our poets, it seems, can sometimes defy the rules of this game, reaching where no spokesperson or scholar has reached. Still, they perform a solely ornamental function. Academics use

Palestinian poets to aestheticize their research; they are placed in the epigraphs of nonfiction books that rely heavily on Israeli and Western scholarship. Perhaps the obvious example here would be Mahmoud Darwish, the most quoted Palestinian poet and one of the most brilliant. Seldom do we encounter the Darwish who tells the colonizers: "Do not pass between us like flying insects. . . . Pile your illusions in a deserted pit, and be gone. . . . Live wherever you like, but do not live among us. . . . Die wherever you like, but do not die among us."[46] Or the Darwish who warns, "But if I hunger, I eat the flesh of my rapist." In fact, that line is often mistranslated. They defang him before they recite him. What is the psychic cost of creating one's self-image through staring at a distorted, manipulated reflection?

ONE MAJOR DANGER IN CONFRONTING THE CONUN-
DRUM OF AUTHORSHIP lies in the temptation to do so with
facile solutions or identitarian shortcuts. Such approaches may
seem like the obvious answer, but oversimplifying an equation,
stripping it of its variables, will ultimately make solving it all the
more convoluted. What is the use of Palestinian talking heads if
they are reciting the same, tired script? What good is a Palestinian in the newsroom when Palestine—both as a geography and
an anticolonial struggle—is nonexistent in the style guide? In
fact, when it is Palestinians who are regurgitating colonial propaganda and racist talking points, refuting them becomes a mud-
dier task. There is a thin line between representation, particularly
liberal reductions around representation, and the reproduction
of the Palestinian as a fetish or a token, thus as a dehumanized
subject once more.

What is worse, as other contexts have shown us, is that
misapprehending identity politics inevitably creates a slippery
slope toward elite capture.[47] Under the guise of progress, super-
ficial inclusion allows entrenched powers to maintain control
in a perpetual and profitable status quo. Our movement's radical demands and our people's basic needs are then diluted into
toothless reforms in the service of Western and even Palestinian
elite interests. As the death toll rises in Gaza, and as Palestinian and pro-Palestinian knowledge producers in the West are
increasingly censured and criminalized, there remain limited
but real niches in which Palestine is emerging as a currency for
social capital nonetheless. The savvy and the sinister can easily
exploit such a phenomenon, not to push for structural change

or collective emancipation but to achieve individualist victories at the expense of the underprivileged classes who are unable to game the system in the same way.

In order to tackle the question of authorship, we must be loyal to the Palestinian street. It is not lost on me that I am running the risk of appealing to populism by using language such as "loyal to the Palestinian street," and the risk of subscribing to the same identity politics I have just denounced. But what I am demanding here is a commitment to a material analysis of the Palestinian question, a learned understanding that is informed by the very streets where the breaking news takes place, by the very people whose slain bodies feature prominently in our documentaries and news reports, but whose experience and expertise are sidelined to make room for Western sources.

Critiquing media and higher education corporations that act as bullhorns for our enemies and boycotting them if need be is only part of the task—the challenge is elevating our own journalistic and academic initiatives. Of course, there is corruption, gatekeeping, and a staggering lack of resources. However, "underdeveloped" is not the only term to describe our infrastructure. It is also creative. Stubborn. Unaffiliated. For instance, citizen journalists in the besieged Gaza Strip—who are usually treated as "fixers" by their international colleagues—have shifted the global narrative and have done so mainly without institutional backing: one, by bypassing the bureaucratic hurdles of legacy media, and two, by decreasing the psychic distance between the subjects of the news, the reporters of the news, and the consumers of the news. We can and should create a practice

MIRACULOUS EPIPHANIES

167

that is rooted in dignity: where we are not trying to convince the butcher to drop their knife, as we have for the past decades; where critical viewership and critical readership are essential; and where the Palestinian is not just a strategic object in a film or an article but a sovereign protagonist whose real story, no matter how it is received by foreign audiences, is reported accurately. Our testimonies have heft, whether published on Israeli websites or not. Our tragedies are real, regardless of whether they are broadcast. Above all, the Palestinian struggle for liberation is heroic—no qualifiers needed. We must not wait for *Haaretz* or the *New York Times* to arrive at the miraculous epiphanies we have long called common truths. We should purge their prestige in our minds, the prestige that renders a *Times* acknowledgment of an eyewitness account more valuable than the account itself.

There are many ways to describe what I am demanding: decolonizing the press or controlling the means of production. Though one could ascribe to it the reductive, identity-focused approach that says "Nothing about us without us," for me it is a lot simpler. Engaging in knowledge production rooted in respect for oneself, one's people, and one's craft. It is about artists and advocates refusing to become state secretaries.[48] It is about storytellers triumphing over that boring formula, escaping the colonial gaze. It is about us talking to each other.

I SHOULD CLARIFY THAT I AM NOT SAYING we should no longer utilize Western sources, nor am I asking non-Palestinian writers to refrain from writing about Palestine. I also understand the allure of the spontaneous, deranged rants of Israeli public figures and the genocidal journals of Zionist pioneers. And I recognize that Israeli journalists and filmmakers often have unparalleled access to archives, sometimes of stolen Palestinian documents, that Palestinians cannot dream of viewing and to interviewees who would laugh at us if we tried to solicit them. The appeal of anti-Zionist Jews sharing their stories of indoctrination is not lost on me either, given that the communities they hail from are often too anti-Palestinian to listen to actual Palestinians.

However, the racism of these communities must be confronted head-on. If one intends to derive credibility from their or their subjects' race, religious identity, or nationality, one has a political duty to make clear their rationale for weaponizing such identity politics. To say explicitly: We cite the settlers' epiphanies not because they are miraculous but because the audience rejects hearing, let alone meaningfully engaging, Palestinians. We quote the talk show host celebrating the massive number of martyrs in Gaza because the American citizen and the American president alike slander the Palestinian Ministry of Health's credibility. To disclose: We are instrumentalizing footage that has been obtained through access journalism. We are betting on our racial privilege. We reference the Israeli genocide scholar because they are Israeli first. The political duty I refer to involves deregulating the racist structures that elevate one testimony over

MIRACULOUS EPIPHANIES

another on a purely identitarian basis—to name them, challenge them, and refuse to perpetuate them.

Simply put, I am asking for a little humility. Western knowledge producers or those using Western voices in their knowledge production should ask themselves a few questions: Where do Palestinians fit in this work? Do they have any agency, or are they a tool to drive the point across? Are my filmmaking practices extractive? How can I practice responsible authorship? Have I instilled in my project enough cues to incentivize my audience to consume it critically, or am I patting myself on the back? Am I doing the challenging chore of speaking to my bigoted, acrimonious community, accosting my Zionist aunt at the dinner table, or am I preaching—pandering, really—to the choir? Did I really have to go and "see for myself," or did I ignore a century of Palestinian literature? Am I cognizant of how that refusal to engage local and grassroots knowledge production continues to undermine its value on the world stage, undermining also the value and authority of Palestinian narration? Do I have a class analysis in my work? Do I acknowledge that I get awards for saying similar things to what the student movement has been criminalized, suspended, and censured for saying? Do I name my institutional backing? What are the material and monetary conditions of those whose voices I amplify? Am I only referencing dead guys? What does my works cited page look like?

▼

8.   *are we indeed all palestinians?*

> *It was the time to hear things and talk . . .*
> *now the sun and the bossman were gone . . .*
> —Zora Neale Hurston[1]

THE STENOGRAPHER PARTY TOOK place inside a fancy Manhattan building, and those in attendance, I imagined, ate veal and aggressively patted each other on the back. Congratulations were due, and I, with other writers and journalists, over a hundred of them, waited outside to deliver. The ceremony was supposed to be over by 9:30 p.m., but the honorable guests, likely aware of our presence, were slow to leave. We were kept company by the NYPD's counterterrorism patrol. It was ten-something when they reluctantly began to exit, dressed in tuxedos and cocktail dresses, and we welcomed them with a few chants, my favorite: "Do your job, tell the truth!"

It was outlandish, I thought, that the 2023 Committee to Protect Journalists' International Press Freedom Awards were hosted by the *New York Times*—the same institution that issued an editorial against a ceasefire in Gaza as the Israeli occupation forces, at the time of our protest, had killed thirty-seven Palestinian journalists and one Lebanese cameraman. (The number at the time of this writing is 175).[2] I eventually came to the conclusion that it was not outlandish but rather a sensible, albeit sardonic, metaphor for journalism in the West. The metaphor expanded when I began to see several journalists, so unmistakably Muslim, walking in and out of the gala. It was as if their presence, like Obama's in the White House, debunked the allegations of systemic racism in the institution. I would lock eyes with a few of them. A few offered me smiles I can only describe as awkward and fled the scene.

I do not want to cast judgment as to why they did not join our ranks. Perhaps it was a nervous reflex or loss of face or the absence of a warm invitation on our end. Perhaps they are elsewhere, politically speaking. Maybe some wanted to participate in the protests but ultimately believed it to be bad optics to pick up one of the posters shaming the *Times*'s editorial board and chant alongside us. Who knows. Protest movements are generally revered in the past tense, once their radical demands become a boring norm. In real time, though, they are led by killjoys and looters who don't understand that there's a time and a place.

Is it cynical to assume that, when deciding to invite Muslim guests, the *New York Times* gave equal weight to their professional merit as they did to their religious and racial identities? Muslim representation at such a dinner, at such a time of heightened distrust of press corporations, could signal that the chants about racism and complicity are baseless—if there were any truth in these accusations, the Muslims and the Arabs

ARE WE INDEED ALL PALESTINIANS? 173

would surely have boycotted the stenographer party. Now, such a party becomes a metric, separating the angry journalists from the reasonable, serious journalists who might criticize the *Times* occasionally but do it with couth.

I too would like to have my cake and eat it. However, there is dissonance, a discrediting dissonance, in indulging institutions that we accuse of bias and complicity. It makes those of us who take a principled stance, who say, *We will not engage until you cease your omissions and fabrications, until you stop coddling our oppressors with passive voice, until you dismantle your dehumanizing standards, until you treat us as trustworthy equals* look like naive teenagers. Naive to reject the golden ticket, the validation and platitudes. Naive to reject the readership of millions, even if such readership requires that editors mutilate our voices beyond recognition. I understand the lure of a mainstream embrace. Beyond the attention, it pays rent and then some.

We tell ourselves it isn't careerist aspirations that drive us to the stenographer party; rather, we want to change things from the inside. We enter these rooms and pander—and are pandered to—to secure a seat at the table. It is for good reason that we shed our skin to assimilate into the world that invisibilizes us: after acquiring respectability and protection, we will finally wear our real faces. But we quickly learn that the inside is already rotten, and we too run the risk of decay. Once we have institutional protection, we'll want to stay protected. And once we get some money, we'll want more wealth. When we go back to ourselves after a long career and look deep in our closets for the skin we once wore, we find it shriveled and discolored, foreign to us as we are foreign to it. One could say it is strategic—but we know what the master's tools will not do.

Mainstream media institutions, whose approval we so desperately seek, will never accept us as their own. They will not absolve us. Beyond the microaggressions, censure, and editing us while we sleep, if the opportunity arises, they will even give cover to the villains in our stories. And they have. When Israeli forces killed Issam Abdallah,* who was reporting in South Lebanon, the media behaved as it usually does, parroting official Israeli state narratives and obfuscating what eyewitnesses and local journalists reported. Even Reuters, Abdallah's employer, refused to name the Israeli military as the culprit until weeks after his killing.† Our likeness, whether on a roster, a masthead, or in between quotation marks, is a currency in this identity-abusing world, and it is exploited to legitimize and diversify these complicit establishments, to shield them against accusations of bias and racism while abandoning us when push comes to shove, when the handcuffs are slapped on our wrists.

Some might argue that some proximity to the institution is better than none. There is truth in the claim that affiliations with respected publications or affluent organizations may afford us slightly more protection against persecution. But at what cost? Is

---

* Issam Abdallah (1986–2023) was a Lebanese video journalist. On October 13, 2023, Abdallah was killed on the job by Israeli tank fire in South Lebanon.

† On October 29, Reuters acknowledged Abdullah was killed by a strike "from the direction of the Israeli border," citing an investigation by Reporters Without Borders. "RSF Initial Report: Reuters Journalist Was Killed in Lebanon in 'Targeted' Strike," Reuters, October 29, 2024.

the world that we want to live in a world where our incarceration will only make noise if we are spectacular people by Western standards, with bylines in high-brow magazines and résumés riddled with American and European recognition?

THEY APPREHENDED OMAR AT THE AIRPORT, and that, my friend told me, was the "silver lining." He knew they were coming for him, but he was terrified they would break in and snatch him from his bedroom, which is more traumatizing than being arrested during the routine though humiliating questioning one has come to expect upon landing in Tel Aviv. Omar will be behind bars, in administrative detention, without charge or trial, for the next four months. Technically, I should write "for the next four months *at least*" because the incarceration order is indefinitely renewable, but I cannot bear thinking of that heartbreaking possibility, let alone what they might have done to him, or are doing.

"There is nothing that we can do," other friends said when I suggested we campaign for his release. When one becomes an administrative detainee—again, held hostage without charge or trial—no amount of public pressure can influence the military commander to rescind his decision. "Not [even] the Hague."[3]

Besides, he would have despised the optics of posters, protests, and social media posts dedicated solely to him, as he hates the inevitable individuality of such campaigns. Though, in terms of the qualifications necessary to seduce a Western audience into solidarity, he possesses them all: the unique story, the respectable résumé, the saintly character. But thousands in Zionist dungeons face the same unknown fate. And hundreds of thousands of entire lives, not just liberty, were decimated, pulverized in the last few months. Most of them nameless, most of them unsung. Singular stories, especially when told recklessly, tend to isolate the individual from the group, sanctifying the former and demonizing the latter. Singular stories tend to situate man-made atrocities outside of politics, reinventing them as inexplicable natural disasters. Omar was imprisoned precisely because he refused such singularity. Since his charges remain undisclosed, per the protocols of the prison, I can speculate that it was his resolute presence on the streets, during protests and jail support, that put him in the enemy's field of vision.

When Ramallah slept or was drugged or anesthetized into political paralysis, Omar was among the few hundred who were awake in the dormant city, chanting, shouting, and sending desperate smoke signals, telling Gaza, *You are not alone*. Our land's mutilated geography could not separate him (and those with him, those he was with) from the rest of our people. His eyes were watching over Gaza, only pausing to glare at those looking away.

He would have refused to distract from those surviving on animal feed or stitching their loved ones' limbs onto their stolen bodies; his arrest is only a symptom of a much more menacing condition. That too was a silver lining. Believing this, digesting this moral and political clarity, is easier on the stomach than conceding to one's own powerlessness or, worse, one's own sordid spinelessness.

178   PERFECT VICTIMS

IT WAS A FEW YEARS AGO, ON THE STREETS OF RAMALLAH, when the city was alert and flouncing, that I made a morbid joke. Nizar Banat, a dissident political leader of some sorts had just been killed by a special unit of the Palestinian Authority security forces.* Thousands of us were protesting and getting beaten up with Palestinian batons. The tear gas used by PA forces in Ramallah was painfully reminiscent of the tear gas that Israeli police deploys against us in Jerusalem. (The connection between the two forces, of course, is not symbolic. The special unit responsible for killing Banat obtained Israeli permission to cross from an "Area A" in Ramallah to an "Area C" in Hebron where he resided to murder him. Much like the police, intelligence, and civil defense bodies funded and trained by the US and several European countries, this PA unit carries out its functions in collaboration with its Israeli counterparts. "Sacred" was the word Mahmoud Abbas used to describe his shameful collaboration with the colonizer, what he calls "security coordination.")

"Raise, raise, raise your voice," we were chanting, "those who chant do not die!" "Ironically," I turned to my friend, "he died *because* he chanted." I don't know what to do with brutality except to laugh at it. My friend was not amused. Nizar died because he was alone, she scolded me. My comment was, in a way, a vulgar allusion to Amal Dunqul's line,

---

* The security forces of the Palestinian Authority were established as part of the Oslo accords in the mid-1990s.

I hang from the morning's gallows
and my forehead is lowered by death
because alive, I did not lower it.[4]

Dunqul seemed to insinuate that the hangman would only spare those burrowing their heads in the sand.

"They can't kill us all," she said. If everyone—lawyers, doctors, grocers, business owners, professors, custodians, car dealers, dope dealers—were chanting, the argument goes, nothing could kill us, not the American-made tear gas thrown at us by PA security forces, nor the bullets, also American, fired at us by soldiers donning the Star of David on their fatigues. Whether that is true—that "the people united will never be defeated"—is yet to be seen. What is true, unnervingly, undoubtedly, is that our conundrum is not about victory or defeat; rather, it is about the simple fact that there is no excuse for us to hide in our safe silences while our siblings are slaughtered. How bitter, how shameful is survival if won only in solitude?

ARE WE INDEED ALL PALESTINIANS, in our thousands and millions, as we chant on the streets of New York and London?* I have been asking myself that question, incessantly, obsessively. Two years ago I would have said, declared even, that the cement of the Israeli military barriers is just that, cement, and the only weight it holds is symbolic. Their colonial borders, try as they might, do not and could not sever the social and national ties keeping our isolated towns together. Our different papers—travel documents, passports, laissez-passers, or lack thereof—are mere words on a page, incapable of dividing us.

Those dispersed behind walls and barbed wire, I would have said, can still unite in their hearts. Yet I walk around these metropoles, protesting—there is repression, though no tear gas yet—and Omar is in a cell in one of the Occupation's prisons, in which at least sixty Palestinian political prisoners have been martyred since October 7.[5] In Khan Yunis, men in tracksuits are shot in the chest, in the head, in the courage of their last action, be it running toward an armored Merkava† or running away to relative safety. In Beirut's Shatila refugee camp, a grandfather lives and dies haunted by visions of his old house by the beach, so visceral he could almost smell the sea. In Jerusalem, I worry about my family's house, about my brother on his commute to work and the trigger-happy police. Other places might as well

---

* I have no issue with the protest chant itself; I think it is rather beautiful.

† Meaning chariot or throne in Hebrew, the Merkava is a series of main battle tanks used exclusively by the Israeli occupation forces. It is considered one of the best armored machines among weapons of war across the globe.

be other planets, each with their own leading cause of death.

In the Naqab, Palestinian Bedouins are uprooted and replaced by German pine trees. In Silwan, the occupation forces demolish homes to fulfill a biblical fantasy. In Sheikh Jarrah, ethnic cleansing comes disguised as a "real-estate dispute." In Beita, settlers build outposts on hilltops, soldiers alongside them. In Masafer Yatta, an Israeli supreme court judge—himself a settler in the occupied West Bank—rules to expel some thousands of Palestinians from their ancestral lands, which they have inhabited and cultivated for generations. Out of all the loot, the Land remains—indisputably—the most valuable.

The Israeli regime's architecture of displacement uses many different methods, but all have a single goal: to control as much land as possible while keeping as few Palestinians as possible, without triggering international alarm bells—be it through manufacturing "real-estate disputes"; demolishing homes built "without authorization"; stealing lands by declaring them "military zones," "archaeological sites," "environmentally protected," or "state-owned"; or simply by stunting the growth of Palestinian communities by isolating them and severing their social and economic ties with neighboring towns. The Zionist project has always created narratives to legalize and justify replacing the native with the settler.[6]

If you're driving across the length of our bruised geography you will at various points encounter rubble. Sometimes it is the rubble of a house in Jerusalem, demolished once or more than once, in the past few decades. Other times, it is the ruins of a village, depopulated in 1948 and now poorly concealed under a forest of pine trees planted by the Jewish National Fund. Sometimes it is the rubble of a bullet-strafed home in the occupied Syrian Golan, which came to its knees during the 1967 invasion. Other times, it is the rubble of a residential building bombed during one of the assaults on the besieged Gaza Strip—in 2008, '09, '12, '14, '19, or '21, or today. Or, if you are reading this a few years from now, it may well be the wreckage of Silwan, Masafer Yatta, and the Naqab, towns that are still bustling but threatened.

As you breeze through this landscape, you will likely come across towns and refugee camps with posters of our martyrs pinned all over the walls. The dates on some of the posters may be difficult to decipher, but you can guess when they were first plastered by looking at their condition: if they are pristine and vibrant, they're fresh off the press; if brittle and faded, damaged by rain, dirt, or stray bullets, and peeling off the walls, they might be from some time ago—the Second Intifada or one of the Intifadas that came after. Many, likely most, of the faces will be unfamiliar to you, for they have been killed outside the international news cycle—their deaths marked only by fleeting local headlines. If you slow down to read, you might find portraits of a father and a son sharing the same wall, an uncle and a niece, sometimes from the same year, sometimes generations apart.

For Palestinians, the Nakba is relentless and recurring. It happens in the present tense—and it happens everywhere on the map. Not a corner of our geography is spared, not a generation since the 1940s. For my own family, the Nakba was my grandmother's experience of expulsion from Haifa by the Haganah in

1948—but it was also her cautionary tales warning me of what would inevitably be my fate when army-backed settlers with Brooklyn accents took over half of my home in Sheikh Jarrah in 2009, declaring my house their own by divine decree. For other families, the Nakba began when a beloved grandmother was expelled from Jaffa and sought refuge in Gaza—where it continues in the rumble of the warplanes dropping bombs on overcrowded refugee camps, introducing her grandchildren to their first (or perhaps third or sixth) war. It is their faces on the posters that are yet to be printed.[7]

Fragmentation is not merely symbolic; it has transformed us into a million people living in a million states at once. Some of us are starving, some of us are well-fed. Some are unemployables, others ascend in rank. One segment of our society, what remains of it anyway, has paid a steeper, bloodier price than the rest in recent years, a detail one cannot simply gloss over. Once upon a time, I could easily estrange myself from the classes that I have long despised and envied, the elites, the bourgeoises, and those for whom Palestine is an aesthetic metaphor. But a new class has emerged in the narrow inferno of the Gaza Strip: the starved and the repeatedly, relentlessly, implacably dispossessed, and it is impossible to be more than an impotent spectator, impossible to belong to that class, not without bruises, not without sacrifice.

It is tempting, almost comforting, particularly as I look at the food on my table and the roof over my head, to indulge in guilt, but it is an unproductive sentiment; it does not start revolutions. Guilt imposes itself like a nagging cavity; you are acutely aware of its presence, but you continue to shovel the same sweets into your mouth, until your teeth rot, until you self-destruct.

These days I am haunted by a subtler though deadlier refrain, an unwanted realization: Gaza has the right to forsake us, to never forgive us, to spit in our faces. How many wars has it confronted? How many martyrs has it given? How many bodies were stolen from it, snatched from their fathers' embrace? And how many of us stutter when asked about resistance, or disavow our right to resist entirely, our *need* to resist? How many of us choose our careers over our kin? How many of us could have done something, anything, and did not?

ARE WE INDEED ALL PALESTINIANS?

SINCE OCTOBER 7, MANY PUBLIC FIGURES, MANY OF THEM PALESTINIAN, especially in the West, have reconsidered, even renounced, the catharsis they felt upon viewing the images of "Palestinian bulldozers" tearing down parts of the Israeli fence encircling Gaza. (I put "Palestinian bulldozers" in quotes because it is an unbelievable phrase.) Many have regretted celebrating the paragliders escaping their concentration camp. One wonders whether the latent apologies were calculated business moves.

The Western world, with its prominent cultural and academic institutions, rejected Gaza's upheaval against the siege, and it demanded that our intelligentsia act accordingly. We were commanded to uphold the status quo (a status quo many of us have built our careers critiquing discursively) in order to maintain our positions, our access, our reputations as the "good ones." Submission to the colonial logic that vilifies the violence of the oppressed and turns a blind eye to the oppressor's violence became the price of admission. Some paid it without hesitation; others struggled as they did it.

Or perhaps this phenomenon is more innocent than cunning careerism, perhaps we are simply afraid. Fear is all around us. It has infested newsrooms and campuses and invaded our apartments and places of worship. It has forced us to mutter under our breath the words we should chant. Those of us who stand with "the children of darkness" will be blackmailed and blacklisted. "Either you are with us or with the terrorists," bosses and world leaders say to those who listen, planting fear in their hearts.

Are these anxieties based on real threats? Or has the enemy succeeded in using its fear-mongering policies to stifle the masses? What is that fear, anyway, compared to the fear of dying of starvation, of being flattened under a military tank, of being suffocated under the wreckage, of being the lone survivor of your family, of your heart breaking for the millionth time? What is that fear if not theater?

I too am afraid. When I heard the news about Omar, many told me I should not go back home or else I would also be in handcuffs. But even from my glass house, I can say with certainty there is no room for fear or silence.

ARE WE INDEED ALL PALESTINIANS?

SO HERE WE ARE IN THE FINAL HOUR, if there was ever one. The task is difficult, or difficult to define. And I'm not preaching from a pulpit, but speaking while suffocating under the weight of my own helplessness, trying to understand what I should do, trying to understand *what* it is that I am doing. I am often asked, in interviews and on university campuses, what role I think literature plays in the Palestinian liberation movement. And though the question itself is not subversive, it certainly feels that way: What *is* the role of literature? Who does it serve, here, in the English-speaking world, in fancy hotel lobbies and fancy college auditoriums, planets away from the makeshift rifles of the refugee camps? It is hard to say. It is hard to imagine what a poem can do in the barrel of a gun.

For some time now, I have been dragging my friends into enervating debates about my dilemma. What is the role of cultural production in a liberation struggle, in our liberation struggle to be exact? A friend of mine, a political organizer, told me that "art cannot exist for art's sake," that it must serve a greater purpose in the struggle. Another friend, a singer, argued that artists are more effective when they convey individualized narratives rather than what he called "the abstracted slogans of the cause." Another said she believes in the rifle and nothing but the rifle. Others pointed to some of the great poets and writers who crafted the discourse that I regurgitate today, and asked how I can be a cynic and a parrot at the same time.

Usually, I offer my standard anecdote: Rashid Hussein wrote his sardonic poem "God Is a Refugee" in protest of the 1960 Israeli Land Law, which prohibits the selling or transfer

188   PERFECT VICTIMS

of "state-owned" lands (as in 93 percent of all lands seized in 1948), and the 1950 Absentee Property Law, which allowed the Israeli government to arrogate the properties of Palestinian refugees dispossessed during the Nakba. His poem not only documented Zionist land theft but helped catalyze the farmers and landowners toward launching a general strike. Etcetera. I provide the easy answers: artists raise awareness globally and fuel the masses locally.

This is certainly true for Zionism, which, in Ghassan Kanafani's words, "employed [literature] extensively not only for its propaganda efforts but for its political and military campaigns as well."[8] Zionist literature's "disciplined march to the rhythm of the political movement, as it crescendo[ed] from novel to novel, and from story to story," certainly served its colonial project in Palestine.[9] Artists, writers, intellectuals, diplomats, journalists, academics, those operating in the public sphere, can and have influenced international public opinion in many instances across history. But sometimes, I'm tempted to say otherwise. I'm tempted to say that it's all smoke and mirrors, that after all the poems and essays and speeches, there is not a dent in the status quo.

It's becoming increasingly difficult to resist that temptation. The more I'm accoladed with adjectives for my writing, the more I'm reminded that such accolades are oversized and meaningless, especially as others receive no such recognition having suffered—and continuing to suffer—behind bars and in hospital beds, having sacrificed their limbs or even their lives. And especially as the perfunctory "existence is resistance" sentiment remains en vogue.* Make no mistake, Mahfoutha Shtayyeh's existence, as she clings on to her olive trees in the face of bulldozers, is resistance. The existence of Palestinians confronting expulsion in Silwan, Sheikh Jarrah, and Masafer Yatta, confronting erasure in Lebanon's refugee camps, etcetera, is resistance. But what about those among us who have more mobility and access? How can our contributions transcend symbolic identitarian gestures? Again, it's hard to imagine what a poem can do in the barrel of a gun.

---

* This is not to be confused with Existence Is Resistance, the organization.

I HEAR THE PHRASE *WE MUST HONOR OUR MAR-TYRS,* but what does it look like to truly *honor* them? Witnessing, whatever that may mean, is not enough, at least not on its own. Nor is it enough to honor them with discursive lullabies and empty, pseudo-radical slogans. I am repeatedly reminded of the late Bassel al-Araj's words, "If you want to be an intellectual, you have to be engaged"—though I am inclined to argue the Arabic word for "engaged," *mushtabik*, carries a much more militant connotation—"If you don't want to be engaged, if you don't want to confront oppression, your role as an intellectual is pointless."[10]

The rallying cry that *We are all Palestinians* must abandon the metaphor and manifest materially. Meaning, all of us—Palestinians or otherwise—must embody the Palestinian condition, the condition of resistance and refusal, in the lives we lead and the company we keep. Meaning we reject our complicity in this bloodshed and our inertia when confronted with all of that blood. Meaning Gaza cannot stand alone in sacrifice.

But the task is difficult. Can we defeat Zionism and end its monstrous reign? It is even more difficult to define: fragmentation means that different things are asked of us in different locales. We face disparate challenges and circumstances. Can we reverse the effects of fragmentation? Collective struggle seems impossible in a hyper-capitalist, hyper-surveilled world. Unscrupulous logic tells us political discipline is an ineffective weapon, that our efforts are in vain. And personal sacrifices (quitting a job, self-immolation, the thousands of things in between) might feel futile, because they crush the doer while barely denting the status quo.

But this is not about their status quo. It is about ours. It is about our relationship with ourselves and our communities. The few moments of reflection before drifting to sleep, the brief encounter with the mirror in the morning, when we ask ourselves: What are the pretenses that absolve us from participating in history?

Here we are, on different planets, in different realities. Statements that include "should" or "must" run the risk of being disparaging and short-sighted. Yet I cannot help but think that this consequential moment calls on us to raise the ceiling of what is permissible, that it demands that we renew our commitment to the truth, to spitting the truth, unflinchingly, unabashedly, *cleverly*, no matter in what conference room, no matter in whose face. Such bravery is asked of us now, not when gardens grow over our martyrs' graves, not when the debris is swept up and sculpted into memorials, and not when the bloodied press vests of our fallen journalists rest eternally in shadow boxes. Those of us with platforms, with some level of protection, with some social capital or actual capital, must dare to shift culture and not only talk about the necessity of shifting culture. Because Gaza cannot fight the empire on its own. Or, to use an embittered proverb my grandmother used to mutter at the evening news, "They asked the Pharaoh, 'Who made you a pharaoh?' He replied, 'No one stopped me.'"

▼

9. *"do you want to throw israelis into the sea?"*

From the side of refusal, a beautiful morning will rise.
—Mahdi Amel[1]

IN 1973, A BRITISH PARLIAMENTARIAN NAMED CHRISTOPHER MAYHEW promised a five-thousand-pound reward to anyone able to prove that Egypt's second president, Gamal Abdel Nasser, had indeed declared his intent to "drive the Jews into the sea."[2] Mayhew then expanded his criteria to include any documentation of genocidal statements made by a responsible Arab leader. Whatever quotations he received he deemed inauthentic. It was not long before one claimant, a 22-year-old Jewish student, sued Mayhew and their dispute went to the High Court.[3] The case was dropped after the student's lawyer admitted that the statement his client provided, a quote from the first secretary-general of the Arab League, "was not genocidal."[4]

Mayhew called the trope "apocryphal."[5] Still, apocryphal as it may be, I am often asked if I want to throw Israelis into the sea. This question has persisted for decades, leveled as an accusation against Palestinians and allies of our cause. Almost every time, anywhere I take the stage, it is an expected though unwanted guest. Whether I am singing my usual nagging refrain about Zionism or talking to an auditorium about the "creative process" (i.e., stimulants and sedatives), someone will spring from their seat, tripping over themself to ask that million-dollar question, waiting to see if my answer will confirm their bias. To report more accurately, I am asked *why* I want to throw Israelis into the sea, not *if.* That I possess such genocidal intent is already assumed. Not so much an inquiry; rather, it is an attempt to implicate me in the inquisitor's worldview. A worldview where I am a savage, pathologically murderous Arab.

"Israelis" and "Jews" are usually used interchangeably by those posing the question and understood, irrefutably, as interchangeable. The responsibility to then make a pristine distinction between the two falls on me. The burden of pedagogy. But none of those words—"if," "why," "Israelis," "Jews"—is what interests me the most. None of those words play the starring role in that sentence. It is the word "want" that is most telling. Wanting is neither policy nor procedure, neither present nor material. Wanting is hoping, longing. Colonial logic says that if I were to have that mere *desire* within my heart; if I am *fantasizing* about cartoonish revenges, that alone negates my claim to justice. Thus, any testimony of the injustices I have witnessed and endured is unreliable. The brutality of colonialism, the very brutality that is institutionalized and legalized, can then be excused or even warranted, if I were to *want* such a turn of events. Such desires, according to mind-reading critics, linger deep within our psyche and should discredit the Palestinian. Our yearnings impugn our plight. The trouble here is not that our enemies employ this illicit tactic (that is what enemies do) but that we submit to it. We attempt to refute defamation instead of repudiating it. We placate this fallacious logic instead of saying: *Even if*—even if!— *my dreams were your worst nightmares, who are you to rob me of my sleep?*

To simply imagine Palestine without settlers, to simply imagine a sky without drones—that, in the Zionist imagination, is genocidal. If you stick with the "want" of the charge, the notion that *Palestinians want to kill all Jews*, you find that Zionism is at war with our future. It is at war with our ability to articulate, even if only through poems and protest chants, a future in which Zionism does not reign. For in the past one hundred years, Zionism has situated us in a condition of constant dispossession and premature death; our Nakba remains and renews. We are besieged in an inescapable, eternal present tense.

But in his dreams, the Palestinian who lives landlocked near the sea, unable to swim in it due to checkpoints, who has spent years tormented by its salty humidity visiting his kitchen in the summer, tormented by old photographs of his grandparents' house that still stands on the shore, that Palestinian swims in the Mediterranean, declaring, "This sea is mine."[6] In her dreams, the Palestinian walks from Bethlehem to Jerusalem uninterrupted, picking prickly pears on her way, humming, "This sea

196 PERFECT VICTIMS

air is mine."[7] In my dreams, I return to Palestine of the future.* I return to "what was mine: my yesterday. / What will be mine: the distant tomorrow."[8] There are no sirens, no settlers, no strip searches under the streetlights, and I do not stop to wonder why. That, in the Zionist imagination, is genocide.

---

* The late Walid Daqqa once said in an interview:

> I do not want to return to the Palestine of the past, Mandatory Palestine, where the cactus, pomegranates, and water mills are, because simply it only exists in memory. When Palestine becomes romantic, the Right of Return becomes utopian, and this romanticization of return distances us from return itself. I want to return to the Palestine of the future, in which the collective national identity must mirror the geography of the entire homeland. The Oslo accords gave up part of the homeland in exchange for the state, and its signatories replaced Return with the story of return. Return, in this sense, was folkloric. . . . This linguistic swelling expresses the inability to liberate the prisoners, so, in this sense, I long for the homeland or the memory that we will create. I long for the future, for the home I will build. There I will rearrange memory in a place of my choosing.

بيروت حمود، «الأسير منذ ٣٤ عاماً وليد دقة: أوسلو قسّم الفلسطينيين وشعبنا سيحاكم هذه القيادة،» الأخبار، ١١/ نيسان/٢٠١٩

THE IRONY OF SUCH COLONIAL PROJECTIONS IS NOT LOST ON ME. Not only because it is the Israelis who are in fact committing a televised genocide but also because, out of the countless genocidal remarks made by Israeli officials in recent months, plenty have invoked the sea. Recently, Netanyahu reportedly advocated for using the temporary "pier" built by the Pentagon on the shore of Gaza to forcibly transfer Palestinians to other countries.[9] Weeks before that, the Israeli minister for the advancement of the status of women said to a nodding TV anchor, "I don't care about Gaza, I literally don't care. For all I care, they can go out and just swim in the sea. I want to see dead bodies of terrorists around Gaza. That's what I want to see."[10] In 1992, Rabin,* the West's beloved "Soldier of Peace," said, "I would like Gaza to sink into the sea." I could flood the next few pages with similar quotes.

One instinct might be to argue that every accusation is a confession. Another is to neatly show that the colonizer and colonized are governed by two sets of rules—what would the diplomatic response be if, say, Mahmoud Abbas said those words?† What would happen to a Palestinian's career and reputation should they sing the same tune? What free speech? The duplicity is glaring. But pointing out double standards, albeit an effective tool of radicalization, is not a sustainable, long-term political program. And do their words matter when their policies speak for themselves?

---

* Yitzhak Rabin in Jerusalem, September 1992, to a delegation from the Washington Institute for Near East Policy.

† It is hard to imagine him saying anything of such vigor, really.

198 PERFECT VICTIMS

I do not rank Zionist rhetoric high up on my list of priorities. I do not have an interest in restricting the psychic allowance of the Israeli public. *Whatever helps them sleep at night.* That our enemies serenade their children with myths to help them survive their neighboring nightmare, us, is not my concern. I do not care if I am a "human animal" in Israeli folk tales, or if they dream about drowning me in the Mediterranean. My concern is that they have the power to actualize their fantasies, fables, and theology. They have the tools to transform them into a macabre reality, much like they have done in the besieged Gaza Strip. I only care about their dreams because they have taken them to the Knesset.*

We are, after all, the villains in their stories, the fabric of their nightmares. For we exist in opposing universes: In ours, they have razed our homes and looted our towns, transformed us into populations of refugees and amputees. In theirs, we have acted senselessly, stabbing settlers and kidnapping soldiers. We have rained rockets on their prosperous, fenced-off colonies. The question of our motives is obsolete. Why their prosperous colonies are surrounded by poverty is a question I doubt they ever ask

---

* "If a white man wants to lynch me, that's his problem. If he has the power to lynch me, that's my problem," and "Racism is not a question of attitude; it's a question of power. Racism gets its power from capitalism. Thus, if you're anti-racist, whether you know it or not, you must be anti-capitalist. The power for racism, the power for sexism, comes from capitalism, not an attitude." Kwame Ture, in response to a student's question after a talk at Federal City College (now the University of the District of Columbia), in October 1968.

"DO YOU WANT TO THROW ISRAELIS INTO THE SEA?" 199

themselves or one another. The settler is self-deluded. The settler's gaze ignores the ruins atop which the settler town is built. Always in the settler's peripheral vision, rubble is both ubiquitous and unobtrusive, filtered out like our eyes do our noses.

In the Zionist imagination, we are the aggressors, the invaders. And while Ben-Gurion* can say to his disciples, "Let us not ignore the truth among ourselves . . . politically we are the aggressors and they defend themselves. . . . The country is theirs,"[11] most Israelis, raised on a different chorus, do ignore the truth among themselves. They believe Palestine is theirs by divine decree and we, "the children of darkness," have stolen it from them. This aphorism, absurd and ahistorical as it may be, is not weakened by the truth—it exists despite it.

---

* David Ben-Gurion (1886–1973), born David Grün, was a Polish Jew who is considered one of the national founders of the Zionist state. He was the first Israeli prime minister and held office from 1955 to 1963.

PALESTINIANS WERE INVENTED IN THE 1960S BY YASSER ARAFAT to be a thorn in Jews' side, or so the saying goes. *Israel is defending itself* is another mythological parable.[12] While such a claim is silly to me, it is sacred to many. Thus, it would seem unwise to smirk. Mocking false convictions often strengthens them, some argue. When you tell a believer that their idol is inanimate, the stone of the idol turns to flesh before their eyes. What is suppressed festers; what is silenced grows louder; psychological reactance, and so on. But there are two holes in this argument: One, even with the best will, belief is far less deterministic and impartial and far more malleable than we would like for it to be. Two, this argument assumes that the person hurling such aspersions is the intended audience of my response. But such individuals, whose telepathic abilities entitle them to call me genocidal, who believe that I am part of a fake, invented people, are not going to have a change of heart if proven wrong. Certainly not in the auditorium where his enemy is speaking. Certainly not when their goal is chaos, not reconciliation.

Even if we take into consideration the possibility that the provocateurs in the crowd genuinely believe the bullshit they are spewing, we drastically underestimate how personal incredulity, cherry-picking, and confirmation bias distort how the indoctrinated receive, classify, and retain information. We forget that belief has little to do with truth. People tend to believe the powerful, the compelling, not the sincere. The truth, that which is factual and historically accurate, is irrelevant in the face of the dominant, institutionally mainstreamed narratives that forge their truth. "Conquerors, my son, consider as true history only what they have themselves fabricated."[13]

When confronting leading or loaded questions on a public stage, it is imperative to remember that there is an audience to address: all kinds of people—curious, sympathetic, skeptical, receptive, on-the-fence—People whom you need to speak to with both words and body language. One option is to accept that you have been charged and stand trial. Plead your case before this self-appointed judge, gesturing at the dossiers of exonerating evidence you have prepared, hoping for acquittal. Another option is to reject his jurisdiction and to reject the premise that you are a defendant, to refuse to live any more of your life in cross-examination.

AGAIN, I AM OFTEN ASKED IF I WANT TO "THROW ISRAELIS INTO THE SEA." My answer has become increasingly facetious, even flippant. "If they are so afraid of drowning why don't they learn how to swim?" Sometimes I get gasps, occasionally a muffled snicker, and other times, unabridged laughter. After the joke comes the thesis: such questions are red herrings and straw man fallacies asked in bad faith. I obviously believe in freedom and dignity for all, etcetera. Those asking, *What happens to the settlers?* have not once thought about the fate of the six million Palestinian refugees agonizing in exile. This is not so much a polemic but an observation, a fatigued observation, reiterated incessantly. Such distracting questions feed the discursive loop that prioritizes the settlers' theoretical future over our material present that is already marked with extermination.

As Steven Salaita writes, "The question 'but what about the Israelis?' presents itself as innocent, perhaps even crucial, but its underlying rhetoric is insidious. . . . It informs the audience that Zionism must be affirmed before the Palestinian can speak of liberation."[14] As such, the decision to answer a derailing question becomes a political act: Should I take the bait? Should I skip over the tanks that set our neighborhoods ablaze, the fires engulfing Khan Yunis to extinguish hypothetical flames? Should I forget about the wells they have poisoned,[15] the waters they have arrogated[16] to quench an imaginary thirst? Lately, I just scoff at the question.

But why laugh at a flammable question when I know my words will be twisted and turned upside down? Why make snarky remarks in front of thousands, many of whom might, on

"DO YOU WANT TO THROW ISRAELIS INTO THE SEA?"   203

a subconscious level, already be suspicious of me? Because, most important, it is funny. It feels good to laugh, to ridicule the ridiculous. It is said we use humor to cope, to experience a sense of relief, and so on. I could cite Freud, but my grandmother said it more eloquently: "If we don't laugh, we cry." However, laughter, like other behaviorally contagious phenomena, has historically played a role in influencing people's attitudes and interpretations toward social and political issues. If we move beyond the reductive idea that the humor of the oppressed is merely a "defense mechanism," we can reveal its strategic advantage and transformative potential.

On stage, on television, whenever I talk about the brutality of Zionism and the genocide it is waging against Palestinians, I routinely come across assertions like, *A second Holocaust is afoot* and *the Jews are afraid.** Such postulations act as a gag order, a muzzle, and conversations become whispers. Although there are numerous people who experience profound cognitive dissonance in the face of brazen colonial projection, most feel that they lack the language or necessary audacity for rebuttal. After all, no one wants to be accused of "blood libel." Here, facetious or flippant responses—irreverence at large, really—become pedagogical.

So deride liars who throw rocks and hide their hands; deride manipulators who exploit taboos and tragedies to maintain a

---

* On the one hand, in the United States, "44% of Jewish students do not feel safe on their own campus." On the other hand, there are no universities left in Gaza because they were all destroyed by the Israeli occupation forces. See Scholars Against the War on Palestine, "International Actions Against Scholasticide."

monopoly on violence, who craft their words to extract an urgent, penitent reverence out of you. Derision, in this context, teaches those who share your frustrations that they should not be shamed into accepting an upside-down world. Instead, it acts as a catalyst for critical thinking and intellectual autonomy, empowering the audience to question the status quo, to satirize it, to strip it naked before its yes-men and sycophants.

Here, irreverence subverts the terms of engagement and rearranges the topics of discussion in accordance with their moral or political weight. It does more than merely disrupt the flow of conversation; it actively reconfigures the hierarchy of what deserves outrage—the serious, the consequential—forcing a reevaluation of priorities. Or, in other words, irreverence "functions at the level of unseating previously established patterns of power—it works to move the morally trivial from equal status with the truly serious."[17]

SOME OF MY FRIENDS, PARTICULARLY THE UPWARDLY MOBILE PALESTINIANS among them, are often dismayed with my caustic approach. It is not as amusing to them but terrifying, and I can understand why. As Palestinians, our every civic engagement becomes a public trial. Our every utterance is a test of character. We are always one error away from transforming into terrorists. I misspoke at a march in London some time ago and that simple slip-up became tabloid headlines and led to the Metropolitan police investigating me for terrorism. Vague and broadly defined "anti-terror" laws have translated into a far-reaching crackdown on political advocacy, nationalist expression, and anticolonial speech, so much so that virtually anything can be interpreted as "incitement" or "material support for terrorism."*

For the Arab in the West, the task is to carefully detonate presumptions or suffer their explosions. We must measurably show, before all else, our distance from the charges lodged at us. We need to prove, in the face of preposterous hostility, that we are respectable civilians, journalists, medics, and professors who "are not like Hamas." One blunder is enough to give credence to the rumors that haunt us. The numbers of casualties we

---

* "Material support laws are the black box of domestic terrorism prosecutions, a shape-shifting space into which all sorts of constitutionally protected activities can be thrown and classified as suspect, if not criminal. Their vagueness is key. They criminalize guilt by association and often use political and religious beliefs to demonstrate intent and state of mind." Theoharis, "US Citizen's Solitary Confinement."

report? Inflated. Our tragedies? Orchestrated in "Pallywood."[18] Our mutilated children, incinerated by Israeli warplanes? Dolls used as war propaganda.

So we write our books and make our films knowing that anything we say—seriously or in jest, even anything we imply—can and will be used against us in the courts of law and public opinion. We talk to each other as if the sniper is standing over our shoulder. And I understand the impulse to self-censor. I know that as Palestinians our notoriety precedes us; we are guilty until proven otherwise and otherwise is often impossible. I know that I probably do not resemble myself in most people's imaginations. But there are vast universes outside of the sniper's gaze, worlds beyond the colonizer's field of vision. What matters more than how we will be viewed by our enemies or our allies is how we view one another and what we inspire in one another. Is it self-respect or self-reproach?

To be irreverent at the podium is to remind yourself that you are part of a collective, a scrutinized people whose psychic and affective allowances are shrinking endlessly; the working classes, the exhausted, the under-resourced, those who do not have access to Ivy Leagues or a knack for double-speak. And in that performance of irreverence, you enmesh yourself in their complexities, you make room for them in the public discourse, no matter how they articulate themselves, and you reassign the blame from the victim to the perpetrator. Otherwise, we would be punching down—we would save ourselves and ascend in our careers by throwing others under the bus. For one to be described as *genteel*, someone else needs to be viewed as savage.

Who among our enemies is given the microphone? Government officials, whose remarks, by virtue of their positions, are often featured in the introductory paragraphs of news articles. And who among us is allowed to speak? Most of the time, it is the bereaved, the dispossessed, and the vulnerable, those who are thrust into the domain of advocacy in spite of themselves and individually transformed into one-person media ministries, without perfect scripts or institutional backing.

I am not flippant because of contrarian tendencies or for the entertainment value. I am flippant because I realize that the majority of the Palestinian People do not possess the capacity or desire to coddle ethnocentric values and racist attitudes. Where, in the warzone, would I find the space to alter our vocabulary? And why should I want to? Why would I want to search in our dreams for an indicting lucidity? Or comb through our colloquialisms looking to filter out the uncouth? Again, why should I bypass the fires engulfing our cities to extinguish hypothetical flames?

PERFECT VICTIMS

A PALESTINIAN MAN WALKS HOME IN THE WAR-ZONE. There are sirens and explosions in the distance and a military tank outside of his home. He approaches the Israeli soldier in the armored vehicle and scolds him: "How many times did I tell you not to park your tank in my driveway?" Here, the man has created for himself a realm in which the mighty Merkava is but a boring nuisance, a bureaucratic measure, like doing your taxes. In this realm, the soldier's domination does not permeate into the psyche, his rifle is but a toy gun, and the tear gas in the air is just someone's nauseating perfume.

In other words, irreverence is a dignifying act of refusal, for those confined by siege or incarceration can be emancipated in the mind. To dig a tunnel, one must first imagine it before clawing at the floor. Irreverence builds an alternative reality where the occupation is not impenetrable and the occupier is not indelible. The police officer is not all-knowing nor is the sniper omnipresent. Here the symbolic meaning of military barriers does not extend beyond the tangibility of their cement.[19] For the speaker (the young activist, the academic, or the taxi driver), irreverence is not just a rhetorical strategy but a form of self-preservation and defiance, a stubborn rejection of psychological subjugation. Irreverence is the discursive equivalent of standing tall. I am grateful for the opportunity to be flippant, to satirize and ridicule my seemingly invincible colonizers—to belittle them, to banish them outside of my inner monologues, to turn them into a punchline.

I know that the price of a joke is volatile. Sometimes it is libel, censure, harassment, even handcuffs. Other times, it is free. But

"DO YOU WANT TO THROW ISRAELIS INTO THE SEA?" 209

that latitude, rare as it may be, is worth the gamble. In this realm, laughter is akin to faith in its ability to make wounds hurt a little less. Although I did not explore it much in this book, I have found solace in humor. I have found in it an agency, a mobility, a life. And much like faith consoles a bereaved mother by promising that her slain child, who has been blown to bits, is actually whole, in a better place, a martyr in heaven, laughter brings that better place to earth.

The choice to be irreverent at the podium liberates both the speaker and their audience, albeit briefly. In the pause between the laughter that follows a sardonic observation, something sacred takes place in the unconscious. The grand stage becomes an intimate living room, and the tragedy at hand, whatever it may be, becomes a family affair. The speaker exiles the prestige of the podium from his mind, discarding the role he was coerced into rehearsing, proclaiming what he had been taught to whisper. The spectators are, for a moment, implicated in the spectacle, polluted by its imperfections, in on the joke. Something sacred occurs in the unconscious: a world without pretenses where we look each other in the eye.

▼

epilogue   *rain is coming*

I READ THAT IN GAZA THEY HAVE OPENED A NEW KINDERGARTEN in the north, a phoenix of sorts, and I want to believe that there is already a clean scent of jasmine that follows the teachers as they go about their day. What, if not jasmine, can ease the nagging of children and the nagging of warplanes? I have been holding on to this piece of good news for the past couple of weeks, filling in the blanks with my own speculations. There is jasmine because seeds do not need permission, or a ceasefire, to germinate. Children nag because that is what children do. What do five-year-olds learn, besides the numbers and alphabet, in the time of genocide? What jokes do they tell to pass the hours? Their vocabulary expands, naturally, to include words more brutal than "invasion," "siege," and "Nakba," and their teachers, I imagine, tell them that the past pales in comparison to Gaza's present. Even the rich, those who have not fled, are in tents this time around.

But there is, and always has been, more to our reality. We are, without a doubt, subjects of conquest and colonization, products of circumstance, but we are also so much more than that. At every turn of our bloodied history, we have been brutalized, bereaved, dispossessed, exiled, starved, slaughtered, and imprisoned, but we have, to the world's dismay, refused to submit. For every massacre and invasion, there have been and there are now men and women who pick up their weapons, makeshift and sophisticated—Molotovs, rifles, slingshots, rockets—to fight. There has always been struggle, there has always been jasmine.

In parallel, there is also more to our enemy. Zionism, behind the facade of the impenetrable superpower it purports to be, is more vulnerable today than ever. And I do not say this naively: I do not ask that we gloss over our enemy's capabilities or the power of the empires and mercenaries that back it. Nor do I ask that we trivialize the crushing weight of hundreds of thousands of martyrs or glamorize the men confronting tanks in tracksuits and burden them with more than they can handle. Freedom fighters understand that their opponent is Goliath, that the odds are stacked against them, that they do not have an option but to pick up the stone. But this is a new dawn. Through close inspection—watching state media, listening to the shifting global narrative, witnessing the renaissance of radical movements, even reading the inscriptions in random airport bathrooms—one discovers that this is a new dawn. Zionism may remain a formidable opponent, but it is also an aging, trembling beast, blinded by its own significance, unpredictable as it may be. Sometimes it pounces on you and pierces its fangs in your flesh. Other times it is but a paper tiger.

And it is this discovery that not only shatters the myth of colonial invincibility but but also reminds us that liberation is attainable, the future is within reach. Amid the unrelenting airstrikes and the havoc of demolished cities, it might seem

EPILOGUE: RAIN IS COMING   213

frivolous to fixate on the blossoming jasmine. But we owe it
ourselves to look at everything, to look for everything. To see
the picture with all of its details. As deadly and treacherous and
unrelenting as it is, the Nakba will not last forever. The world is
changing because it must. If seeds can germinate in the inferno,
so can revolution. On the phone, my mother tells me, *rain is
coming and God is almighty.*

▼

"الغيث آتٍ، والله قادر على كل شيء"

acknowledgments

An earlier, shorter version of *Perfect Victims and the Politics of Appeal* was delivered as an Edward Said Memorial Lecture at Princeton University in February 2023. An excerpt from the lecture was later printed as the cover story in a December issue of the *Nation*. The foundational argument of the book, in its most preliminary forms, was presented as a keynote speech at Tufts University's Decolonizing International Relations Conference in October 2021, in a conversation at Harvard Law School in that same month, and as a talk at Bard College's Center for Human Rights and the Arts in March 2022 that was subsequently published in *The Lawlessness of Rights* (CHRA, 2024). In October 2023, I was set to give another iteration of Perfect Victims at the University of Vermont as part of the Will Miller Social Justice Lecture Series, but the university cited "safety concerns" as pretext to move the event off campus or cancel it altogether. Despite the abrupt format change, the lecture was live streamed and viewed by eleven thousand people.

Finishing this book certainly took a village. I am grateful to Haymarket Books, especially Brekhna Aftab, the editor of this manuscript, who has offered me patience and guidance throughout what was a difficult and unpredictable writing process; to Naomi Murakawa and Anthony Arnove for suggesting that I elaborate on my Princeton lecture in a book; to the rest of the

Haymarket team—Rachel, Katy, Myles, Róisín, Aricka, Dana, Julie, Jim, John, and others— and to my agent, Ian Bonaparte, who landed the book in the right hands. I extend my deepest gratitude to my dear friend Amany Khalifa, who has challenged my thinking since I was a teen. I am also grateful for the years and years of feedback from Lizzy Ratner at the *Nation*, for my time working with Adam Horowitz and the rest of the staff at *Mondoweiss*, for Amna Ali, whose assistance throughout this project has been lifesaving, and for Maha Essid and her encouragement and feedback. This book was thoroughly fact-checked by the very discerning and brilliant Karen Ng and generously line-edited once more by Rami Karim, who has long edited my writing.

I am humbled by the openness and grace of my dear friends Ru'a Rimawi and Ahmed al-Naouq, who have allowed me to write, or attempt to write, slivers of their and their loved ones' stories into this book, elevating its value endlessly. I am also indebted to Maisara Baroud, the incredible illustrator whose art, created amid the backdrop of makeshift refugee camps in Rafah, Deir el-Balah, and elsewhere, under the barrage of rockets, has inspired me in countless ways. I am thankful for the many friends and comrades—too numerous to name—whose insights, critiques, and edits have profoundly deepened my thinking and research: Hazem Jamjoum, Ali Almossawi, Abdel Jawad Omar, aja monet, Alia Al-Sabi, Tamar Ghabin, Azad Essa, Rahi M., Nour Annan, Zoé Samudzi, Yasmin El-Rifae, Morgan Bassichis, Rebecca Abou-Chedid, Parin Behrooz, Nihal El Aasar, Lama al-Arian, and many more who I hope will forgive me if I have forgotten to name them. I am also deeply appreciative of

ACKNOWLEDGMENTS 217

the conversations that propelled and sharpened my arguments, especially with Omar Karimah, Samira Esmair, Jonathan Kubakundimana, Raeda Taha, Sulafa Zidani, Molly Crabapple, Hala Marshood, Fayrouz Sharqawi, Bissan Oweidah, Randa Wehbe, Izziddin Mustafa, Idriss Khalidi, Dimitri Shreckengost, Savana Ogburn, Josh Winston, Derecka Purnell, and countless others who I hope will forgive if I have failed to mention them.

Additionally, I thank those who contributed to this book with sources, facts, archival material, disagreements, challenges, and edits to previously published essays, and those who simply lent a listening ear or pointed me in the right direction: Alaa Al-Dayeh, Ahmad Hammad, Tarek Z. Ismail, Riya Alsana, Emma Alpert, Laura al-Bast, Mariam Barghouti, Ahmed Biqawi, Nadi Saadeh, Yazan Nagi, Noura Erakat, Julia Bacha, Jessica Devaney, Tarek Bakri, Jack Mirkinson, Musa al-Sada, Matt Kannarad, Zena Al Tahhan, Bayan Kiwan, Nicki Kattoura, Xavier Dominic, Elana Comay del Junco, Daliah Merzaban, Samer Khuwariah, David Renton, Alastair Lyon, Phoebe Cook, and many, many, many others who I am sure I am forgetting—I am writing this in a rush, but I am truly grateful for everyone who has contributed to this project in any capacity. I also thank Zahid R. Chaudhary and Princeton's english department for the invitation and the hospitality at Princeton. I am also grateful to the CHRA's Tania El Khoury and Ziad Abu-Rish and all who were involved in setting up the event at Bard, to Harvard's International Human Rights Clinic, as well as Isaac Kreisman and Anne Petermann of the Will Miller Social Justice Lecture Series.

Last but not least, I owe a debt of gratitude to my family for their understanding and support, even when I nearly became an absent son and sibling during the writing of this book, especially my beloved twin sister Muna.

works cited

Abbas, Mahmoud. Speech at the Eleventh Session of the Fatah Revolutionary Council, August 24, 2023.

Abdulrahim, Raja, and Ben Hubbard. "A Trailblazing Palestinian Journalist Dies, Aged 51." *New York Times*, May 11, 2022.

Abufarha, Nasser. *The Making of a Human Bomb: An Ethnography of Palestinian Resistance*. Durham, NC: Duke University Press, 2009.

Abunimah, Ali. "How Obama Learned to Love Israel." *Electronic Intifada*, March 4, 2007.

Akram, Fares. "In Rubble of Gaza Seaside Cafe, Hunt for Victims Who Had Come for Soccer." *New York Times*, July 10, 2014.

Ali, Amna. Conversation with author, September 5, 2024.

Ali, Taha Muhammad. *So What: New & Selected Poems (with a Story), 1971–2005*, translated by Peter Cole, Yahya Hijazi, and Gabriel Levin. Port Townsend, WA: Copper Canyon Press, 2006.

Amel, Mahdi. "The Revolutionary War in Lebanon Is Our Universe." *Al-Tariq Magazine*, August 24, 1982.

Amnesty International. "Ukraine: Ukrainian Fighting Tactics Endanger Civilians." August 4, 2022.

Azriel, Guy. "Exclusive: Saudis Say Normalization with Israel 'Matter of Time.'" i24 News, December 6, 2022.

Bacha, Julia, and Rebekah Wingbert-Jabi, dir. *My Neighbourhood*. Just Vision, 2012.

Baldwin, James. "Letter from a Region in My Mind." *New Yorker*, November 9, 1962.

Baldwin, James. "Many Thousands Gone." In *Notes of a Native Son*. Boston: Beacon Press, 1955.

Baldwin, James. "Negroes Are Anti-Semitic Because They're Anti-White." *New York Times*, 1967.

Barghouti, Mariam. "'We Are Living in Graves, and Our Demand Is Freedom': The Gilboa Prison Break One Year Later." *Mondoweiss*, September 9, 2022.

Barghouti, Mourid. *I Saw Ramallah*, translated by Ahdaf Soueif. Cairo: American University in Cairo Press, 2000. First published in Arabic in 1997.

"Basic Law: Israel – The Nation State of the Jewish People." Unofficial translation, Adalah, July 25, 2018.

ben-Tekoa, Sha'i. "Sticks and Stones." *Commentary*, September 2000.

Ben-Yair, Michael. "The War's Seventh Day." *Haaretz*, March 3, 2002.

Berger, Miriam, Evan Hill, and Hazem Balousha. "Four Fragile Lives Found Ended in Evacuated Gaza Hospital." *Washington Post*, December 3, 2023.

Black, Ian. "Doctor Admits Israeli Pathologists Harvested Organs without Consent." *Guardian*, December 21, 2009.

Bulos, Nabih. "Kyiv Civilians Take Up Arms . . . to Fight Russian Attack on Ukraine." *Los Angeles Times*, February 26, 2022.

Burman, Erica. "Fanon and the Child: Pedagogies of Subjectification and Transformation." *Curriculum Inquiry* 46, no. 3 (2016).

Carlstrom, Gregg. "Autopsy Shows Palestinian Teen 'Burned Alive.'" Al Jazeera, July 6, 2014.

Césaire, Aimé. *Discourse on Colonialism*, translated by Joan Pinkham. New York: Monthly Review Press, 2001.

Chomsky, Noam. *The Fateful Triangle: The United States, Israel and the Palestinians*. Boston: South End Press, 1983.

Cordall, Simon Speakman. "'Everything Is Legitimate': Israeli Leaders Defend Soldiers Accused of Rape." Al Jazeera, August 9. 2024.

Cotton, Tom. Interview by Shannon Bream. *FOX News Sunday*, Fox News, October 15, 2023.

Daqqa, Walid. *The Oil's Secret Tale*. Tamer Institute for Community Education, 2018.

Daqqa, Walid. "A Place without a Door," translated by Dalia Taha, Middle East Research and Information Project, July 11, 2023.

Daqqa, Walid. "Uncle, Give Me a Cigarette," translated by Dalia Taha. Middle East Research and Information Project, July 11, 2023.

Darwish, Mahmoud. *Mural*, translated by John Berger and Rema Hammami. New York: Verso, 2017. First published in Arabic in 2000.

Darwish, Mahmoud. "Those Who Pass Between Fleeting Words." *Middle East Report* 154 (September/October 1988).

Darwish, Mahmoud. *Unfortunately, It Was Paradise: Selected Poems*, edited and translated by Munir Akash and Carolyn Forché. Oakland: University of California Press, 2003.

Davies, Harry, et al. "'The Grey Zone': How IDF Views Some Journalists in Gaza as Legitimate Targets." *Guardian*, June 25, 2024.

Decolonize Palestine. "Myth: Israel Is Defending Itself."

Decolonize Palestine. "Myth: Palestinians Fake Israeli Atrocities."

Defense for Children International - Palestine. "Israeli Forces Kill Two Palestinian Children in Early Days of New Year." January 3, 2023.

Defense for Children International - Palestine. "Israeli Forces Use Palestinian Girl as a Human Shield in Jenin." May 19, 2022.

Defense for Children International - Palestine. "Number of Palestinian Children in Israeli Detention." June 30, 2024.

Democracy Now! "'They Were So Close': Israel Kills Medics Trying to Save Dying 6-Year-Old Hind Rajab." Aired on February 16, 2024.

WORKS CITED

Dichter, Avi. Interview on Channel 12, November 11, 2023.

Dr. Huey P. Newton Foundation. *The Black Panther Party: Service to the People Programs*, edited by David Hilliard. Albuquerque: University of New Mexico Press, 2008.

Dunqul, Amal. "The Last Words of Spartacus." In *The Complete Works*. Beirut: Dar al-Shorouk, (1969) 2012.

Dunqul, Amal. "Waiting for the Sword." In *The Complete Works of Amal Dunqul*, 3rd ed. Cairo: Madbouly Publishing, 1987.

Electronic Intifada. "New York Times Fails to Disclose Jerusalem Bureau Chief's Conflict of Interest." January 25, 2010.

Electronic Intifada. "Palestine in Pictures: September 2023." October 5, 2023.

Erakat, Noura. "The Sovereign Right to Kill: A Critical Appraisal of Israel's Shoot-to-Kill Policy in Gaza." *International Criminal Law Review* 19, no. 5 (October 2019): 783–818.

Essa, Azad. "How a 'Hostile' NYC Hospital Fired an Award-Winning Palestinian-American Nurse." *Middle East Eye*, May 31, 2024.

Euro-Mediterranean Human Rights Monitor. "Gaza: Israeli Army Uses Palestinian Civilians as Human Shields in Its Operation in Shifa Medical Complex and Its Cicinity." March 23, 2024.

Euro-Mediterranean Human Rights Monitor. "Israel Uses Water as a Weapon of Its Genocide in Gaza." July 5, 2024.

Eyes on Israeli Military Courts: A Collective of Observers' Testimonies, second edition. Addameer Prisoner Support and Human Rights Association, 2022.

Fanon, Frantz. *Black Skin, White Masks*, translated by Charles Lam Markmann. London: Pluto Press, 1986. First published in French in 1952.

Fanon, Frantz. "Letter to the Resident Minister." In *Toward the African Revolution: Political Essays*, translated by Haakon Chevalier. New York: Grove Press, 1967.

Fanon, Frantz. *The Wretched of the Earth*, translated by Richard Philcox. New York: Grove Press, 2004. First published in French in 1961.

Federgruen, Awi. "Rock-Throwing by Said Should Not Be Excused." *Columbia Daily Spectator*, September 6, 2000.

Fiacc, Padraic. "Soldiers." in *The Selected Padraic Fiacc*. Belfast: Blackstaff Press, 1979.

G.A. Res. 37/43, Importance of the Universal Realization of the Right of Peoples to Self-Determination and of the Speedy Granting of Independence to Colonial Countries and Peoples for the Effective Guarantee and Observance of Human Rights. December 3, 1982.

Gessen, M. "What We Know about the Weaponization of Sexual Violence on October 7th." *New Yorker*, July 20, 2024.

Golan, May. Interview with *Israel Daily* on ILTV News, February 21, 2024.

Goldberg, Jeffrey. *Prisoners: A Muslim and a Jew across the Middle East Divide*. New York: Alfred A. Knopf, 2006.

Habiby, Emile. *The Secret Life of Saeed: The Pessoptimist*, 1974, translated by Salma

K. Jayyusi and Trevor LeGassick. Northampton, MA: Interlink Books, 2003.

Harari, Yuval Noah. Interview by Christiane Amanpour. *Amanpour*, CNN International, October 12, 2023.

Harari, Yuval Noah. Interview on TV Asahi, October 19, 2023.

Harding, Luke. "'I Haven't Told My Granny': Ukraine's Student Molotov Cocktail-Makers." *Guardian*, February 28, 2022.

Harkov, Lahav. "One-Third of Journalists Killed in Gaza Were Affiliated with Terrorist Groups." *Jewish Insider*, May 17, 2024.

Hartman, Saidiya V. *Scenes of Subjection: Terror, Slavery, and Self-Making in Nineteenth-Century America*. New York: Oxford University Press, 1997.

Hartman, Saidiya, and Frank B. Wilderson, "The Position of the Unthought." *Qui Parle* 13, no. 2 (2003): 183–201.

Hassan, Budour. "The Warmth of Our Sons: Necropolitics, Memory, and the Palestinian Quest for Closure." Jerusalem Legal Aid and Human Rights Center, 2019.

Hassan, Mehdi. "Saying Israel Is Guilty of Apartheid Isn't Antisemitic. Just Ask These Israeli Leaders." MSNBC, May 27, 2021.

HC Deb. (5th ser.) (18 Oct. 1973) (861) col. 462.

Herzog, Isaac. Interview on *Sunday with Laura Kuenssberg*. BBC One, November 12, 2023.

Hockstader, Lee. "Letter from Israel." *Washington Post*, July 12, 2000.

Hoffman, Adina. *My Happiness Bears No Relation to Happiness: A Poet's Life in the Palestinian Century*. New Haven, CT: Yale University Press, 2009.

Hopkins, Valerie, and Thomas Gibbons-Neff. "An Amnesty International Assessment That Ukraine 'Put Civilians in Harm's Way' Stirs Outrage." *New York Times*, August 7, 2022.

Hurston, Zora Neale. *Their Eyes Were Watching God*. 1937; New York: Perennial, (1937) 1990.

Hussaini, Maha. "Palestinian Journalist Killed in Israeli Bombing after Threats to End Gaza Coverage." *Middle East Eye*, October 6, 2024.

Hussein, Muhammad. "Remembering Israel's Killing of Four Children on the Beach in Gaza." *Middle East Monitor*, July 16, 2020.

Hussein, Rashid. "Against." In *I'm the Earth, Don't Deny Me the Rain*. Beirut: Falastin al-Thawra, 1976.

Inlakesh, Robert. "'Kill 'Em All' – US Politicians and Their Genocidal Comments against Palestinian since October 7." *Palestine Chronicle*, May 15, 2024.

International Middle East Media Center. "Palestinian Dies from Serious Wounds in Jenin." September 20, 2023.

Isack, Arielle. "Stealing the Voice of Authority." *Baffler*, April 17, 2024.

Jamjoum, Hazem, ed. "The Jewish National Fund: A Para-State Institution in the Service of Colonialism & Apartheid." *Al-Majdal* 43 (Winter–Spring 2010).

Jamous, Lama. "Lama Jamous' Reporting Defends the Future of Gaza." Interview in *New York War Crimes*, June 19, 2024.

Jarrar, Kareem. Al Jazeera interview. Posted to Instagram on August 31, 2024 by

WORKS CITED   223

Shatha Hanaysha (@shathahanaysha).

Al Jazeera. "Dozens Injured in Israeli Police Attack on Palestinian Funeral." May 17, 2022.

Al Jazeera Staff, "Israeli Forces Kill Palestinian Woman in Occupied West Bank." June 1, 2022.

Al Jazeera. "Israeli Police Arrest and Brand Palestinian with 'Star of David': Report." August 18, 2023.

Al Jazeera. "Israeli Tank Fired at Hind Rajab Family Car from Meters Away: Investigation." June 23, 2024.

Al Jazeera. "Israel's Shifting Narratives on the Killing of Shireen Abu Akleh," September 6, 2022.

Al Jazeera. "Israel's War on Gaza: List of Key Events, Day 169." March 23, 2024.

Al Jazeera. "Palestinian Teen Killed in Israeli Raid in Northern Occupied West Bank." August 22, 2023.

Al Jazeera. "US Congressman Tells Pro-Palestine Activist 'We Should Kill 'em All." February 21, 2024.

Jerusalem Watchman. "No Weapon Formed against Israel Shall Prosper." January 15, 2015.

Jordens, Ann-Mari. "Australian Citizenship: 50 Years of Change." *Australian Law Reform Commission Reform Journal* 5, no. 74 (Autumn 1999): 24–28.

Kanafani, Ghassan. *On Zionist Literature*, translated by Mahmoud Najib. Oxford: Ebb Books, (1967) 2022.

Kanafani, Ghassan. *The Revolution of 1936–1939 in Palestine*, translated by Hazem Jamjoum. New York: 1804 Press, [1972] 2023.

Kanafani, Ghassan. "Thoughts on Change and the 'Blind Language.'" *Alif: Journal of Comparative Poetics* 10 (1990): 137–57.

Kane, Alex. "New Conflict of Interest at NYT Jerusalem Bureau," Fairness and Accuracy in Reporting, May 1, 2012.

Karsner, David. *Debs: His Authorized Life and Letters*. New York: Boni and Liveright, 1919.

Kelly, Meg, et al. "Palestinian Paramedics Said Israel Gave Them Safe Passage to Save a 6-Year-Old Girl in Gaza. They Were All Killed." *Washington Post*, April 16, 2024.

Kerr, Jaren, et al., "Israel Calls for Evacuation of 1mn People in Northern Gaza." *Financial Times*, October 13, 2023.

Kim, Sunnie. "Edward Said Accused of Stoning in South Lebanon." *Columbia Daily Spectator*, July 19, 2000.

Kingsley, Patrick, et al. "How Hamas Is Fighting in Gaza: Tunnels, Traps and Ambushes." *New York Times*, July 13, 2024.

Kingsley, Patrick, and Aaron Boxerman. "Hamas Fails to Make Case That Israel Struck Hospital." *New York Times*, October 22, 2023.

Klion, David. "Jeffrey Goldberg Doesn't Speak for the Jews." *Jewish Currents*, August 2, 2018.

Kramer, Andrew E. "Behind Enemy Lines, Ukrainians Tell Russians 'You Are

Never Safe.'" *New York Times*, August 17, 2022.

El-Kurd, Mohammed. "Alaa on My Mind." *Baffler*, December 7, 2022.

El-Kurd, Mohammed. "Are We Indeed All Palestinians?" *Mondoweiss*, March 13, 2024.

El-Kurd, Mohammed. "Dear President Obama . . . I Hope You Won't Remain Silent." *Guardian*, March 17, 2013.

El-Kurd, Mohammed. "Do I Believe in Violence?" *New Arab*, November 22, 2022.

El-Kurd, Mohammed. "Fifteen-Year-Old Girl Killed for Attempting to Kill a Soldier (with a Nail File), or Context." In *Rifqa*. Chicago, IL: Haymarket Books, 2021.

El-Kurd, Mohammed. "Here in Jerusalem, We Palestinians Are Still Fighting for Our Lives." *Guardian*, July 28, 2021.

El-Kurd, Mohammed. "How the Western Media Missed the Story of Shireen Abu Akleh's Death," *Nation*, May 25, 2022.

El-Kurd, Mohammed. "If They Steal Sheikh Jarrah." *Mada Masr*, February 16, 2021.

El-Kurd, Mohammed. "In Every Corner of Palestine, There Is a Story of Dispossession." *Nation*, March 30, 2022.

El-Kurd, Mohammed. "Israeli Protesters Say They're Defending Freedom. Palestinians Know Better." *Nation*, March 30, 2023.

El-Kurd, Mohammed. "Jewish Settlers Stole My Home, It's Not My Fault They're Jewish." *Mondoweiss*, September 26, 2023.

El-Kurd, Mohammed. "The New Campaign to Smear Palestinian Human Rights Defenders as Terrorists." *Nation*, October 22, 2021.

El-Kurd, Mohammed. "On 'Perfect Victims' and the Politics of Appeal." Edward W. Said Memorial Lecture presented at Princeton University, February 8, 2023.

El-Kurd, Mohammed. "Rain Is Coming: The Ongoing Nakba and the Present Revolution." *New York War Crimes,* May 15, 2024.

El-Kurd, Mohammed. "Refaat al-Areer: An Incomplete Eulogy," Institute for Palestine Studies, January 31, 2024.

El-Kurd, Mohammed. "Reflections on the 75th Anniversary of a Nakba That Never Ended." *Nation*, May 15, 2023.

El-Kurd, Mohammed. "The Stenographer Party." *Mondoweiss*, November 29, 2023.

El-Kurd, Mohammed. "Tomorrow My Family and Neighbors May Be Forced from Our Homes by Israeli Settlers," *Nation*, November 20, 2020.

El-Kurd, Mohammed. "'We Shouldn't Grow Up Dreaming That Our Friends Don't Get Killed.'" *Nation*, February 1, 2023.

El-Kurd, "Western Journalists Have Palestinian Blood on Their Hands." *Nation*, October 20, 2023.

El-Kurd, Mohammed. "What Does It Mean to Be Palestinian Now?" *Nation*, January 25, 2024.

Lacan, Jacques. *The Four Fundamental Concepts of Psychoanalysis: The Seminar of Jacques Lacan*, book 11, edited by Jacques-Alain Miller, translated by Alan Sheridan. New York: W. W. Norton and Company, 1998.

WORKS CITED 225

LeBlanc, John Randolph. *Edward Said on the Prospects of Peace in Palestine and Israel.* New York: Palgrave MacMillan, 2013.

Leonhardt, David, and Lauren Jackson. "Gaza's Vital Tunnels." *New York Times,* October 30, 2023.

Leyens, Jacques-Philippe, et al. "Infra-humanization: The Wall of Group Differences." *Social Issues and Policy Review* 1, no. 1 (December 2007): 139–72.

The Lobby - USA. Season 1, episode 1, "The Covert War." Aired in November 2018 on Al Jazeera English.

Loewenstein, Antony. "How Israel Commodifies Mass Killing throught Its 'Palestine Laboratory.'" Interview by Jeremy Scahill. *Intercepted,* December 13, 2023.

Lorde, Audre. *Sister Outsider.* Berkeley: Crossing Press, 1984.

MacDonald, Alex, and Shatha Hammad. "Shireen Abu Akleh: Arab Journalists Remember Iconic Palestinian Reporter." *Middle East Eye,* May 11, 2022.

Macron, Emmanuel. "Europe speech," Sorbonne University, April 25, 2024.

Makaber al-Arqam (مقابر الأرقام) [Popular National Campaign]. makaberalarqam. ps/en.

Maltz, Judy, "The Lawyer for Jewish Terrorists Who Started Out by Stealing Rabin's Car Emblem," *Haaretz,* January 4, 2016.

Manna, Jumana. "The Embargo on Empathy." *Hyperallergic,* November 1, 2023.

Mateus, Sofia Diogo. "Ukrainians Google 'How to Make a Molotov Cocktail' After Defense Minister's Call to Arms." *Washington Post,* February 25, 2022.

Mathis-Lilley, Ben. "Critics Question Whether Pastor Who Said Hitler Was Sent by God Was Good Choice to Speak at U.S. Embassy in Israel." *Slate,* May 14, 2018.

Al Mayadeen. "IOF Assassinate Zakaria Zubeidi's Son, Others Killed in West Bank." September 5, 2024.

Al Mayadeen. "19-yo Palestinian, Shot, Used as Human Shield, Dies in Israeli Custody." August 26, 2024.

McNeil, Sam. "Israel Deploys Remote-Controlled Robotic Guns in West Bank." Associated Press, November 16, 2022.

Meir, Golda. *A Land of Our Own: An Oral Autobiography,* edited by Marie Syrkin. New York: G. P. Putnam's Sons, 1973.

Mer-Khamis, Juliano, dir. *Arna's Children.* Pieter van Huystee Film and Trabelsi Productions, 2004.

Middle East Eye. "Israeli Forces Kill Palestinian Journalist near West Bank Camp." June 1, 2022.

Middle East Monitor. "Israel Police Brands Palestinian Prisoner's Face with Star of David." August 21, 2023.

Middle East Eye, "Shireen Abu Akleh: New Footage Shows Police Storming Hospital before Funeral." May 16, 2022.

Middle East Monitor. "Symbolic Funeral Held in Nablus as Israel Withholds Bodies of Slain Palestinians." August 29, 2023. Video, 30 sec.

Middle East Eye. "War on Gaza: Netanyahu 'Suggests New US-Built Port Could

Help Deport Palestinians.'" March 20, 2024.

Miller, Stephen Kekoa. "The Importance of Not Being Earnest: The Role of Irreverence in Philosophy and Moral Education." *Metodički ogledi* 30, no. 2 (2019): 32.

Morgenthau, Hans J. *Politics among Nations and the Struggle for Power and Peace.* New York: Alfred A. Knopf, 1948.

Morrison, Toni. Interview on *Charlie Rose*, January 19, 1998.

Mousa, Hanan. "Palestinian Children's Literature: An Overview." *Jeunesse: Young People, Texts, Cultures* 12, no. 1 (2020): 144–159.

Murphy, Maureen Clare. "Israelis Cheer after Palestinian Boy Is Executed in Jerusalem." *Electronic Intifada*, August 31, 2023.

Al-Mutanabbi, Abu Tayyib. "Fidan Laka Man Yuqassiru 'An Madaka." [Publication info TK]

Najib, Mohammed. "Palestine Runs Dry: 'Our Water They Steal and Sell to Us.'" Al Jazeera, July 15, 2021.

Netanyahu, Benjamin. "PM Netanyahu Addresses the 37th Zionist Congress," transcript of speech, Embassy of Israel to the United States, October 20, 2015.

New Arab. "Dumbest Excuse for Occupation: No Letter 'P' in Arabic." February 11, 2016.

New Arab, "Israeli Forces 'Poisoned Wells in Palestinian Villages' during 1948 Nakba, Unearthed Documents Show." October 15, 2022.

New Arab. "Israel Harvesting Organs from Palestinian Bodies, Say Gaza Officials." December 27, 2023.

New Arab, "Palestinian Teen Shot by Israeli Soldiers Near Joseph's Tomb Dies of Injuries." August 19, 2023.

Newsnight. "Israel Vows 'Terrible' Response to Hamas Attack." Aired on October 9, 2023, on BBC News.

Newton, Huey P. *Revolutionary Suicide.* New York: Harcourt Brace Jovanovich, Inc., 1973.

New York War Crimes. "'Words Like Slaughter': A Study of *The New York Times'* Reporting in Ukraine and Gaza." August 20, 2024.

Ofir, Jonathan. "Itamar Ben-Gvir and His Fascist Ilk Inadvertently Advance the Apartheid Discourse." *Mondoweiss*, August 28, 2023.

Olmert, Ehud. Interview with *Haaretz,* 2010.

Omar, Abdaljawad. "The Question of Hamas and the Left." *Mondoweiss*, May 31, 2024.

Osborne, Samuel. "Civilians Help Make Molotov Cocktails to Take On Russian Forces." Sky News, February 27, 2022.

Othman, Orouba. "Reshaping the Victim: On Stealing Shireen Abu Akleh from Her People," translated by Nadine Fattaleh. *7iber*, June 7, 2022.

Palestine News and Information Agency (WAFA). "Two Palestinians, One Minor, Shot and Seriously Injured by Israeli Occupation Forces Overnight in East Jerusalem." August 19, 2023.

Palestinian Information Center. "Ministry of Prisoners: 36 Gazan Prisoners Die of Torture in Israeli Prisons." June 21, 2024.

WORKS CITED

"Palestinian Open Letter," September 11, 2023, https://sites.google.com/view/palestinianopenletter/home?authuser=1%28they.

"Palestinians Are a Thorn [Video]." *JewishPress*. August 18, 2016.

Patel, Yumna. "Israeli Police Attack Another Palestinian Funeral in Jerusalem." *Mondoweiss*, May 17, 2022.

Patai, Raphael, ed. "June 12, 1895," In *The Complete Diaries of Theodor Herzl*, translated by Harry Zohn. New York: Herzl Press and Thomas Yoseloff, 1960.

Perlmutter, Mark. "Children of Gaza," interview on *CBS News Sunday Morning*, July 21, 2024.

Petti, Matthew. "A Fanatical Israeli Settlement Is Funded by New York Suburbanites." *New Lines Magazine*, February 12, 2024.

Protection of Civilians Report, 8–21 August 2023. United Nations Office for the Coordination of Humanitarian Affairs, 2023.

Protection of Civilians Report, 5–18 September 2023. United Nations Office for the Coordination of Humanitarian Affairs, September 26, 2023.

Purnell, Derecka. "Dehumanization, Disability, and Resistance." In *Becoming Abolitionists: Police, Protests, and the Pursuit of Freedom*. New York: Astra House, 2021, 209–43.

Qabbani, Nizar. "Footnotes to the Book of the Setback," stanza 3, translated by Abdullah al-Udhari. *Critical Muslim*.

Reuters. "US and EU Slam Palestinian President's Remarks on Holocaust." September 7, 2023. https://www.reuters.com/world/us-eu-slam-palestinian-presidents-remarks-holocaust-2023-09-07.

Revkin, Andrew C. "My Stroke of Luck." *New York Times*, May 13, 2013.

Robotoro23. "No Electricity, Food, Water or Gas: Israel Orders 'Complete' Gaza Siege." Reddit thread posted on r/stupidpol in September 2023.

Rubio, Marco. Interview by Jake Tapper. *The Lead with Jake Tapper*, CNN, October 9, 2023.

Sabbagh-Khoury, Areej. *Colonizing Palestine: The Zionist Left and the Making of the Palestinian Nakba*. Redwood City, CA: Stanford University Press, 2023.

Said, Edward W. *After the Last Sky: Palestinian Lives*. New York: Columbia University Press, 1999.

Said, Edward W. "Withholding, Avoidance, and Recognition." *Mawaqif* 19–20 (January 1972).

Salaita, Steven. "The Importance of Being Flippant." *Mondoweiss*, May 9, 2022.

Sarkar, Urvashi. "Janna Jihad: Meet Palestine's 10-Year-Old Journalist," Al Jazeera, April 28, 2016.

Scholars Against the War on Palestine. "Toolkit: International Actions Against Scholasticide." February 2024.

Shalhoub-Kevorkian, Nadera. *Incarcerated Childhood and the Politics of Unchilding*. Cambridge: Cambridge University Press, 2019.

Shalhoub-Kevorkian, Nadera, and Sarah Ihmoud. "Two Letters from Jerusalem: Haunted by Our Breathing." *Jerusalem Quarterly* 59 (2014): 8.

Shamas, Diala. "Tax Breaks for Colonization?" The Law and Political Economy

Project, June 30, 2021.

Shoughry-Badarne, Bana. "Torture in Israel: A Question of Getting Away With It." in *On Torture*, 47–54. Adalah, Physicians for Human Rights, and Al Mezan Center for Human Rights, 2012.

Smith, Dinitia. "A Stone's Throw Is a Freudian Slip." *New York Times*, March 10, 2001.

Steinbuch, Yaron. "Heroic Ukrainian Soldier Blows Himself Up on Bridge to Prevent Russian Advance." *New York Post*, February 25, 2022.

Al Tahhan, Zena. "'Devastating': How Israeli Is Pulling Palestinian Families Apart," Al Jazeera, March 15, 2022.

Al Tahhan, Zena. "Elderly Palestinian Man Dies during Arrest by Israeli Army." Al Jazeera, January 12, 2022.

Táíwò, Olúfẹ́mi O. *Elite Capture: How the Powerful Took Over Identity Politics (And Everything Else.* Chicago, Haymarket Books, 2022.

Theoharis, Jeanne. "US Citizen's Solitary Confinement Raises Serious Questions." *Progressive*, March 1, 2010.

Tobin, Andrew. "Israel's Top Security Experts Redraw West Bank Map for the Trump Era." *Jewish Telegraphic Agency*, January 3, 2017.

UK Lawyers for Israel. "Hospital Removes Gaza Artwork from Hospital Corridor." February 14, 2023.

University of Southern California Office of the Provost. "Important Update on 2024 Commencement." April 15, 2024.

Varenikova, Maria. "Hate for Putin's Russia Consumes Ukraine." *New York Times*, March 7, 2022.

Wahbe, Randa May. "The Politics of Karameh: Palestinian Burial Rites under the Gun." *Critique of Anthropology* 40, no. 3 (2020): 323–40.

Weir, Alison. "US Media and Israeli Military: All in the Family," If Americans Knew, February 25, 2010

Weisberg, Hila. "David Brooks: Gaza War Proved My Son Was Right to Serve in IDF." *Haaretz*, October 18, 2014

Weiss, Philip, and Adam Horowitz. "Another New York Times' Reporter's Son Is in the Israeli Army." *Mondoweiss*, October 27, 2014.

Weltsch, Robert. "Mayhew Action Dropped." *AJR* [Association of Jewish Refugees] *Information* 31, no. 4: 3, https://ajr.org.uk/wp-content/uploads/2018/02/1976_april.pdf.

Wiener, Jon. "Obama and the Palestinian Professors." *Nation*, April 10, 2008.

Wilkins, Brett. "'Level the Place,' Declares Lindsey Graham as Israel Does Exactly That to Gaza." *Common Dreams*, October 11, 2023.

Wood, Graeme. "The UN's Gaza Statistics Make No Sense." *Atlantic*, May 17, 2024.

notes

1. the sniper's hands are clean of blood

1. Padraic Fiacc, "Soldiers," in *The Selected Padraic Fiacc* (Belfast: Blackstaff Press, 1979).
2. Portions of this passage appeared in Mohammed El-Kurd, "Are We Indeed All Palestinians?" *Mondoweiss*, March 13, 2024.
3. Nadera Shalhoub-Kevorkian and Sarah Ihmoud, "Two Letters from Jerusalem: Haunted by Our Breathing," *Jerusalem Quarterly* 59 (2014): 8.
4. Gregg Carlstrom, "Autopsy Shows Palestinian Teen 'Burned Alive,'" Al Jazeera, July 6, 2014.
5. "Israeli Tank Fired at Hind Rajab Family Car from Meters Away: Investigation," Al Jazeera, June 23, 2024.
6. Meg Kelly et al., "Palestinian Paramedics Said Israel Gave Them Safe Passage to Save a 6-Year-Old Girl in Gaza. They Were All Killed," *Washington Post*, April 16, 2024.
7. "'They Were So Close': Israel Kills Medics Trying to Save Dying 6-Year-Old Hind Rajab," *Democracy Now!*, February 16, 2024.
8. Al-Mutanabbi, "Fidan Laka Man Yuqassiru 'An Madaka," 354 AH/965 CE. My translation.
9. Husam Zomlot, "Israel Vows 'Terrible' Response to Hamas Attack," interview by Kirsty Wark, *Newsnight*, BBC, October 9, 2023.
10. Zomlot, "Israel Vows."
11. Portions of this passage appeared in Mohammed El-Kurd, "Western Journalists Have Palestinian Blood on Their Hands," *Nation*, October 20, 2023.
12. El-Kurd, "Western Journalists."
13. Sima Vaknin-Gil quoted in *The Lobby - USA*, "The Covert War," episode 1, produced by the Al Jazeera Investigative Unit, 2017.
14. *The Lobby - USA*, "Covert War."
15. Ann-Mari Jordens, "Australian Citizenship: 50 Years of Change," *Australian Law Reform Commission Reform Journal* 5, no. 74 (Autumn 1999): 24–28.
16. Numbers 14:33
17. Parts of this passage were published in Mohammed El-Kurd, "The Right to Speak for Ourselves," *Nation*, December 11/18, 2023.
18. To understand the reality of colonization in Sheikh Jarrah, see Mohammed El-Kurd, "If They Steal Sheikh Jarrah," *Mada Masr*, February 16, 2021; "Here

230 PERFECT VICTIMS

in Jerusalem, We Palestinians Are Still Fighting for Our Lives," *Guardian*, July 28, 2021; "Tomorrow My Family and Neighbors May Be Forced from Our Homes by Israeli Settlers," *Nation*, November 20, 2020.

2. the politics of defanging

1. Jacques Lacan, *The Four Fundamental Concepts of Psychoanalysis: The Seminar of Jacques Lacan*, book 11, 1964, ed. Jacques-Alain Miller, trans. Alan Sheridan (New York: W. W. Norton, 1998), 268.
2. Saidiya Hartman with Frank B. Wilderson, "The Position of the Unthought," *Qui Parle* 13, no. 2 (2003): 183–201.
3. See Derecka Purnell, "Dehumanization, Disability, and Resistance," in *Becoming Abolitionists: Police, Protests, and the Pursuit of Freedom* (New York: Astra House, 2021), 209–43.
4. Quran 17:37.
5. Nasser Abufarha, *The Making of a Human Bomb: An Ethnography of Palestinian Resistance* (Durham, NC: Duke University Press, 2009), 8.
6. Some lines in this section have previously appeared in an Arabic essay titled "Refaat al-Areer: An Incomplete Eulogy," published by the Institute for Palestine Studies on January 31, 2024.
7. Ghassan Kanafani, "Thoughts on Change and the 'Blind Language,'" 1968, trans. Barbara Harlow and Nejd Yaziji, *Alif: Journal of Comparative Poetics* 10 (1990): 148.
8. Kanafani, "Thoughts on Change," 148.
9. Aimé Césaire, *Discourse on Colonialism*, trans. Joan Pinkham (New York: Monthly Review Press, 2001), 74.
10. Mohammed El-Kurd, "Fifteen-Year-Old Girl Killed for Attempting to Kill a Soldier (with a Nail File), or Context," in *Rifqa* (Chicago: Haymarket Books, 2021), 29.
11. Rashid Hussein, "Against," in *I'm the Earth, Don't Deny Me the Rain* (Beirut: Falastin al-Thawra, 1976). My translation.

3. shireen's passport

Portions of this chapter were previously published in Mohammed El-Kurd, "How the Western Media Missed the Story of Shireen Abu Akleh's Death," *Nation*, May 25, 2022.

1. Ephesians 2:8–9.
2. Al Jazeera Staff, "Israeli Forces Kill Palestinian Woman in Occupied West Bank," Al Jazeera, June 1, 2022.
3. Raja Abdulrahim and Ben Hubbard, "A Trailblazing Palestinian Journalist Dies, Aged 51," *New York Times*, May 11, 2022. The headline has since been amended to "Trailblazing Palestinian Journalist Killed in West Bank."
4. *Middle East Eye* Staff, "Shireen Abu Akleh: New Footage Shows Police Storming Hospital before Funeral," *Middle East Eye*, May 16, 2022.

NOTES

5. CBS News (@CBSNews), "Video shows Israeli riot police clashing with mourners at the funeral for Al Jazeera journalist Shireen Abu Akleh, who was killed two days earlier. At one point, the tussling becomes so intense that her coffin almost topples to the ground," Twitter (now X), May 13, 2022, https://x.com/CBSNews/status/1525151546530582528.

6. "Dozens Injured in Israeli Police Attack on Palestinian Funeral," Al Jazeera, May 17, 2022.

7. Yumna Patel, "Israeli Police Attack Another Palestinian Funeral in Jerusalem," *Mondoweiss*, May 17, 2022.

8. Muhammad Hussein, "Remembering Israel's Killing of Four Children on the Beach in Gaza," *Middle East Monitor*, July 16, 2020.

9. *Middle East Eye* Staff, "Israeli Forces Kill Palestinian Journalist near West Bank Camp," *Middle East Eye*, June 1, 2022.

10. Frantz Fanon, *The Wretched of the Earth*, trans. Richard Philcox (1961; New York: Grove Press, 2004), 50.

11. Frantz Fanon, "Letter to the Resident Minister," written in 1956, published in *Toward the African Revolution: Political Essays*, trans. Haakon Chevalier (New York: Grove Press, 1967), 53.

12. Orouba Othman, "Reshaping the Victim: On Stealing Shireen Abu Akleh from Her People," trans. Nadine Fattaleh, *7iber*, June 7, 2022.

13. Othman, "Reshaping the Victim."

14. A version of this passage appeared in Mohammed El-Kurd, "Do I Believe in Violence?" *New Arab*, November 22, 2022.

15. Rashid Hussein, "Against," in *I'm the Earth, Don't Deny Me the Rain* (Beirut: Falastin al-Thawra, 1976). My translation.

16. Parts of the passage appeared in Mohammed El-Kurd, "'We Shouldn't Grow Up Dreaming That Our Friends Don't Get Killed,'" *Nation*, February 1, 2023.

17. Parts of the passage appeared in Mohammed El-Kurd, "The Right to Speak for Ourselves," *Nation*, December 11/18, 2023.

18. Nabih Bulos, "Kyiv Civilians Take Up Arms . . . to Fight Russian Attack on Ukraine," *Los Angeles Times*, February 26, 2022.

19. Sofia Diogo Mateus, "Ukrainians Google 'How to Make a Molotov Cocktail' after Defense Minister's Call to Arms," *Washington Post*, February 25, 2022.

20. Luke Harding, "'I Haven't Told My Granny': Ukraine's Student Molotov Cocktail-Makers," *Guardian*, February 28, 2022.

21. Yaron Steinbuch, "Heroic Ukrainian Soldier Blows Himself Up on Bridge to Prevent Russian Advance," *New York Post*, February 25, 2022.

22. Samuel Osborne, "Civilians Help Make Molotov Cocktails to Take On Russian Forces," Sky News, February 27, 2022.

23. Maria Varenikova, "Hate for Putin's Russia Consumes Ukraine," *New York Times*, March 7, 2022.

24. Andrew E. Kramer, "Behind Enemy Lines, Ukrainians Tell Russians 'You Are Never Safe,'" *New York Times*, August 17, 2022.

25. Patrick Kingsley et al., "How Hamas Is Fighting in Gaza: Tunnels, Traps and

232 PERFECT VICTIMS

Ambushes," *New York Times*, July 13, 2024.
26. Kramer, "Behind Enemy Lines."
27. Kingsley et al., "How Hamas Is Fighting in Gaza."
28. Kramer, "Behind Enemy Lines."
29. Kingsley et al., "How Hamas Is Fighting in Gaza."
30. David Leonhardt and Lauren Jackson, "Gaza's Vital Tunnels," *New York Times*, October 30, 2023.
31. Amnesty International, "Ukraine: Ukrainian Fighting Tactics Endanger Civilians," press release, August 4, 2022.
32. Valerie Hopkins and Thomas Gibbons-Neff, "An Amnesty International Assessment That Ukraine 'Put Civilians in Harm's Way' Stirs Outrage," *New York Times*, August 7, 2022.
33. Hopkins and Gibbons-Neff, "Amnesty International Assessment."
34. Kingsley et al., "How Hamas Is Fighting in Gaza."
35. Emmanuel Macron, speech at Sorbonne University, April 25, 2024.
36. Yuval Noah Harari interview by Christiane Amanpour on *Amanpour*, CNN International, October 12, 2023.
37. Marco Rubio on *The Lead with Jake Tapper*, CNN, October 9, 2023.
38. Quoted in Robert Inlakesh, "'Kill 'Em All' – US Politicians and Their Genocidal Comments against Palestinian since October 7," *Palestine Chronicle*, May 15, 2024.
39. Quoted in Brett Wilkins, "'Level the Place,' Declares Lindsey Graham as Israel Does Exactly That to Gaza," *Common Dreams*, October 11, 2023.
40. Tom Cotton on *FOX News Sunday*, anchored by Shannon Bream, October 15, 2023.
41. "US Congressman Tells Pro-Palestine Activist 'We Should Kill 'em All,'" Al Jazeera, February 21, 2024.
42. Yuval Noah Harari on TV Asahi, October 19, 2023.
43. Harry Davies et al., "'The Grey Zone': How IDF Views Some Journalists in Gaza as Legitimate Targets," *Guardian*, June 25, 2024.
44. Alex MacDonald and Shatha Hammad, "Shireen Abu Akleh: Arab Journalists Remember Iconic Palestinian Reporter," *Middle East Eye*, May 11, 2022.
45. Lahav Harkov, "One-Third of Journalists Killed in Gaza Were Affiliated with Terrorist Groups," *Jewish Insider*, May 17, 2024.
46. Jeffrey Goldberg, *Prisoners: A Muslim and a Jew across the Middle East Divide* (New York: Alfred A. Knopf, 2006), 22–26.
47. David Klion, "Jeffrey Goldberg Doesn't Speak for the Jews," *Jewish Currents*, August 2, 2018.
48. M. Gessen, "What We Know about the Weaponization of Sexual Violence on October 7th," *New Yorker*, July 20, 2024.
49. Philip Weiss and Adam Horowitz, "Another *New York Times* Reporter's Son Is in the Israeli Army," *Mondoweiss*, October 27, 2014.
50. Alex Kane, "New Conflict of Interest at NYT Jerusalem Bureau," Fairness and Accuracy in Reporting, May 1, 2012.

NOTES   233

51. Andrew Tobin, "Israel's Top Security Experts Redraw West Bank Map for the Trump Era," *Jewish Telegraphic Agency*, January 3, 2017.
52. Tobin, "Israel's Top Security Experts."
53. "Israeli Forces Use Palestinian Girl as a Human Shield in Jenin," Defense for Children International - Palestine, May 19, 2022.
54. AlJazeera Arabic, video posted YouTube on May 11, 2022.

4. a life in cross-examination

1. Statement to Judge David C. Westenhaver immediately after Debs was convicted under the Sedition Act of 1918, on September 14, 1918. David Karsner, *Debs, His Authorized Life and Letters* (New York: Boni and Liveright, 1919), 48.
2. Taha Muhammad Ali, "Abd el-Hadi Fights a Superpower," in *So What: New & Selected Poems (with a Story), 1971–2005*, trans. Peter Cole, Yahya Hijazi, and Gabriel Levin (Port Townsend, WA: Copper Canyon Press, 2006), 3–7. My translation.
3. Edward W. Said, "Withholding, Avoidance, and Recognition," *Mawaqif* 19–20 (January 1972). My translation.
4. Edward W. Said, *After the Last Sky: Palestinian Lives* (New York: Columbia University Press, 1999), 17.
5. James Baldwin, "Many Thousands Gone," in *Notes of a Native Son* (Boston: Beacon Press, 1955), 27.
6. Jacques-Philippe Leyens et al., "Infra-humanization: The Wall of Group Differences," *Social Issues and Policy Review* 1, no. 1 (December 2007): 139–72.
7. Hans J. Morgenthau, *Politics among Nations and the Struggle for Power and Peace* (New York: Alfred A. Knopf, 1948), 14.
8. Mourid Barghouti, *I Saw Ramallah*, trans. Ahdaf Soueif (Cairo: American University in Cairo Press, 2000), 178.
9. Mourid Barghouti, *I Saw Ramallah*, 178.
10. Frantz Fanon, *Black Skin, White Masks*, trans. Charles Lam Markmann (London: Pluto Press, 1986), 17–18.
11. "Important Update on 2024 Commencement," University of Southern California Office of the Provost, April 15, 2024.
12. Azad Essa, "How a 'Hostile' NYC Hospital Fired an Award-Winning Palestinian-American Nurse," *Middle East Eye*, May 31, 2024.
13. Aimé Césaire, *Discourse on Colonialism*, trans. Joan Pinkham (New York: Monthly Review Press, 2000), 44.
14. Césaire, *Discourse on Colonialism*, 44.
15. Césaire, *Discourse on Colonialism*, 44.
16. Adina Hoffman, *My Happiness Bears No Relation to Happiness: A Poet's Life in the Palestinian Century* (New Haven, CT: Yale University Press, 2009), 308.
17. Ali, "Abd el-Hadi the Fool," in *So What*. My translation.
18. Ali, "Abd el-Hadi the Fool." My translation.
19. Ali, "Abd el-Hadi the Fool." My translation.

234   PERFECT VICTIMS

5. tropes and drones

A portion of this chapter was previously published in an essay titled "Jewish Settlers Stole My Home, It's Not My Fault They're Jewish," which appeared in *Mondoweiss* on September 26, 2023. The opening paragraph was inspired by James Baldwin, "Negroes Are Anti-Semitic Because They're Anti-White," *New York Times*, April 9, 1967.

1. Baldwin, "Negroes Are Anti-Semitic."

2. Such organizations include the Jewish Agency for Israel, the World Jewish Congress (and its regional constituent Jewish Congresses), the Center for Jewish–Christian Understanding and Cooperation, and the Jewish Power Party. By far the most important Zionist para-state organization with regard to Palestinian land (and its confiscation) is the Jewish National Fund (JNF). For more on the JNF, see the essays collected in Hazem Jamjoum, "The Jewish National Fund: A Para-State Institution in Service of Colonialism & Apartheid," *Al-Majdal* 43 (Winter–Spring 2010).

3. *My Neighbourhood*, directed by Julia Bacha and Rebekah Wingbert-Jabi (Just Vision, 2012).

4. Mohammed El-Kurd (@m7mdkurd), Twitter, November 3, 2021, 12:44 p.m.

5. See Israeli Nation-State Law, Clause 7, Basic Law: Israel as the Nation-State of the Jewish People.

6. Sam McNeil, "Israel Deploys Remote-Controlled Robotic Guns in West Bank," Associated Press, November 16, 2022. See also Antony Loewenstein, "How Israel Commodifies Mass Killing throught Its 'Palestine Laboratory,'" interview by Jeremy Scahill, *Intercepted*, December 13, 2023.

7. Jonathan Ofir, "Itamar Ben-Gvir and His Fascist Ilk Inadvertently Advance the Apartheid Discourse," *Mondoweiss*, August 28, 2023.

8. "Israel Police Brands Palestinian Prisoner's Face with Star of David," *Middle East Monitor*, August 21, 2023.

9. Mahmoud Abbas, speech at the 11th session of the Fatah Revolutionary Council, August 24, 2023. See "US and EU Slam Palestinian President's Remarks on Holocaust," Reuters, September 7, 2023.

10. See "Palestinian Open Letter," September 11, 2023, sites.google.com/view/palestinianopenletter.

11. "Palestinian Open Letter."

12. "Israeli Police Arrest and Brand Palestinian with 'Star of David': Report," Al Jazeera, August 18, 2023.

13. *Protection of Civilians Report, 8–21 August 2023*, United Nations Office for the Coordination of Humanitarian Affairs, August 28, 2023.

14. "Two Palestinians, One Minor, Shot and Seriously Injured by Israeli Occupation Forces Overnight in East Jerusalem," Palestine News and Information Agency (WAFA), August 19, 2023.

15. *New Arab* Staff, "Palestinian Teen Shot by Israeli Soldiers Near Joseph's Tomb Dies of Injuries," *New Arab*, August 19, 2023.

NOTES 235

16. "Israel's War on Gaza: List of Key Events, Day 169," Al Jazeera, March 23, 2024.
17. "Palestinian Teen Killed in Israeli Raid in Northern Occupied West Bank," Al Jazeera, August 22, 2023.
18. "Palestinian Dies from Serious Wounds in Jenin," International Middle East Media Center, September 20, 2023.
19. "Symbolic Funeral Held in Nablus as Israel Withholds Bodies of Slain Palestinians," *Middle East Monitor*, August 29, 2023.
20. *Protection of Civilians Report, 5–18 September 2023*, United Nations Office for the Coordination of Humanitarian Affairs, September 26, 2023.
21. Maureen Clare Murphy, "Israelis Cheer after Palestinian Boy Is Executed in Jerusalem," *Electronic Intifada*, August 31, 2023.
22. "Israeli Forces Kill, Withhold Body of 14-Year-Old Palestinian Boy in Jerusalem," Defense for Children International – Palestine, August 31, 2023.
23. "Israeli Soldier Killed in Car Ramming Attack by Palestinian," Al Jazeera, August 31, 2023.
24. "Palestine in Pictures: September 2023," *Electronic Intifada*, October 5, 2023.
25. *Middle East Eye* Staff, "Israeli Forces Kill Palestinian in West Bank Raid," *Middle East Eye*, September 1, 2023.

6. *mein kampf* in the playroom

1. Isaac Herzog interview on *Sunday with Laura Kuenssberg*, BBC One, November 12, 2023.
2. Herzog interview.
3. "Dumbest Excuse for Occupation: No Letter 'P' in Arabic," *New Arab*, February 11, 2016.
4. "PM Netanyahu Addresses the 37th Zionist Congress," transcript of speech, Embassy of Israel to the United States, October 20, 2015.
5. See "Gaza: Israeli Army Uses Palestinian Civilians as Human Shields in Its Operation in Shifa Medical Complex and Its Vicinity," Euro-Mediterranean Human Rights Monitor, March 23, 2024; "19-yo Palestinian, Shot, Used as Human Shield, Dies in Israeli Custody," *Al Mayadeen*, August 26, 2024.
6. "Israel's Shifting Narratives on the Killing of Shireen Abu Akleh," Al Jazeera, September 6, 2022.
7. A version of this passage was published in Mohammed El-Kurd, "What Does It Mean to Be Palestinian Now?," *Nation*, January 25, 2024.
8. A version of this passage appeared in El-Kurd, "What Does It Mean."
9. David Keyes quoted in *Gaza Fights for Freedom*, directed by Abby Martin (Empire Files, 2019).

7. miraculous epiphanies

1. Lee Hockstader, "Letter from Israel," *Washington Post*, July 12, 2000.
2. Sunnie Kim, "Edward Said Accused of Stoning in South Lebanon," *Columbia Daily Spectator*, July 19, 2000.
3. Miriam Berger, Evan Hill, and Hazem Balousha, "Four Fragile Lives Found

Ended in Evacuated Gaza Hospital," *Washington Post*, December 3, 2023.

4. Awi Federgruen, "Rock-Throwing by Said Should Not Be Excused," *Columbia Daily Spectator*, September 6, 2000.

5. Matthew Petti, "A Fanatical Israeli Settlement Is Funded by New York Suburbanites," *New Lines Magazine*, February 12, 2024; Diala Shamas, "Tax Breaks for Colonization?" Law and Political Economy Project, June 30, 2021.

6. Sha'i ben-Tekoa, "Sticks and Stones," *Commentary*, September 2000.

7. ben-Tekoa, "Sticks and Stones."

8. See Jon Wiener, "Obama and the Palestinian Professors," *Nation*, April 10, 2008; and Ali Abunimah, "How Obama Learned to Love Israel," *Electronic Intifada*, March 4, 2007.

9. Justus Reid Weiner quoted in Hockstader, "Letter from Israel."

10. See Dinitia Smith, "A Stone's Throw Is a Freudian Slip," *New York Times*, March 10, 2001.

11. John Randolph LeBlanc, *Edward Said on the Prospects of Peace in Palestine and Israel* (New York: Palgrave MacMillan, 2013), 90.

12. Quoted in Kim, "Edward Said Accused."

13. LeBlanc, *Edward Said*, 90.

14. Amal Dunqul, "Waiting for the Sword," in The Complete Works of Amal Dunqul, 3rd ed. (Cairo, Madbouly Publishing, 1987), 193. My translation.

15. Mohammed El-Kurd, "The Right to Speak for Ourselves," *Nation*, December 11/18, 2023.

16. A version of this passage was previously published in Mohammed El-Kurd, "Dear President Obama . . . I Hope You Won't Remain Silent," *Guardian*, March 17, 2013.

17. El-Kurd, "Dear President Obama." Italics added.

18. Walid Daqqa, "A Place without a Door," trans. Dalia Taha, Middle East Research and Information Project, July 11, 2023.

19. Daqqa, "A Place without a Door."

20. Walid Daqqa, "Uncle, Give Me a Cigarette," trans. Dalia Taha, Middle East Research and Information Project, July 11, 2023.

21. James Baldwin, "Letter from a Region in My Mind," *New Yorker*, November 9, 1962.

22. After/Inspired by Padraic Fiacc, "Soldiers," in *The Selected Padraic Fiacc*, (Belfast: Blackstaff Press, 1979), 67.

23. Daqqa, "Uncle, Give Me a Cigarette."

24. The Dr. Huey P. Newton Foundation, *The Black Panther Party: Service to the People Programs*, ed. David Hilliard (Albuquerque: University of New Mexico Press, 2008), 8.

25. For more on Palestinian children's literature, see Hanan Mousa, "Palestinian Children's Literature: An Overview," *Jeunesse: Young People, Texts, Cultures* 12, no. 1 (2020): 144–59.

26. Frantz Fanon, *The Wretched of the Earth*, trans. Richard Philcox (1961; New York: Grove Press, 2004), 69.

NOTES

27. After Rashid Hussein, "Against," in *I'm the Earth, Don't Deny Me the Rain* (Beirut: Falastin al-Thawra, 1976). My translation.

28. See Erica Burman, "Fanon and the Child: Pedagogies of Subjectification and Transformation," *Curriculum Inquiry* 46, no. 3 (2016): 3.

29. *Arna's Children*, directed by Juliano Mer-Khamis (Pieter van Huystee Film and Trabelsi Productions, 2004).

30. Mariam Barghouti, "'We Are Living in Graves, and Our Demand Is Freedom': The Gilboa Prison Break One Year Later," *Mondoweiss*, September 9, 2022.

31. The video, in Arabic, is part of Al-Arabiya's archive on YouTube, posted September 14, 2021. (In September 2024, Israeli media revealed direct cooperation of Al-Arabiya with the Israeli army. See "Saudi-Owned Al-Arabiya in Bed with Israeli Army to 'Shape Gaza Coverage': Report," *Cradle*, September 21, 2024.)

32. "IOF Assassinate Zakaria Zubeidi's Son, Others Killed in West Bank," *Al Mayadeen*, September 5, 2024.

33. See Nadera Shalhoub-Kevorkian, *Incarcerated Childhood and the Politics of Unchilding* (Cambridge: Cambridge University Press, 2019).

34. Graeme Wood, "The UN's Gaza Statistics Make No Sense," *Atlantic*, May 17, 2024.

35. Dr. Mark Perlmutter, "Children of Gaza," interview with on *Sunday Morning*, CBS News, July 21, 2024.

36. "Hospital Removes Gaza Artwork from Hospital Corridor," UK Lawyers for Israel, February 14, 2023.

37. Toni Morrison, interview on *Charlie Rose*, January 19, 1998.

38. Arnon Degani, "Israel Is a Settler-Colonial State – and That's OK," *Haaretz*, September 13, 2016.

39. Michael Ben-Yair, "The War's Seventh Day," *Haaretz*, March 3, 2002.

40. "June 12, 1895," in *The Complete Diaries of Theodor Herzl*, ed. Raphael Patai, trans. Harry Zohn (New York: Herzl Press and Thomas Yoseloff, 1960), 1:84.

41. Vladimir Jabotinsky, "The Iron Wall," 1923, quoted in Areej Sabbagh-Khoury, *Colonizing Palestine: The Zionist Left and the Making of the Palestinian Nakba* (Redwood City, CA: Stanford University Press, 2023).

42. Hadas Gold et al., "Israeli Minister Says There Is 'No Such Thing as Palestinian People,' Inviting US Rebuke," CNN, March 21, 2023.

43. A version of this passage was previously published in El-Kurd, "Right to Speak."

44. Mehdi Hassan, "Saying Israel Is Guilty of Apartheid Isn't Antisemitic. Just Ask These Israeli Leaders." MSNBC, May 27, 2021. Emphasis added.

45. Said, *After the Last Sky*, 3.

46. Mahmoud Darwish, "Those Who Pass Between Fleeting Words," *Middle East Report* 154 (September/October 1988).

47. Olúfẹ́mi O. Táíwò, *Elite Capture: How the Powerful Took Over Identity Politics (And Everything Else)* (Chicago: Haymarket Books, 2022).

48. A version of this passage was previously published in Mohammed El-Kurd, "The Stenographer Party," *Mondoweiss*, November 29, 2023.

8. are we indeed all palestinians?

This chapter incorporates portions of two of my essays previously published in *Mondoweiss*, "The Stenographer Party," November 29, 2023, and "Are We Indeed All Palestinians?" March 13, 2024.

1. Zora Neale Hurston, *Their Eyes Were Watching God* (1937; New York: Perennial, 1990), 1.
2. The number of journalists killed, according to Gaza's government media office cited in Maha Hussaini, "Palestinian Journalist Killed in Israeli Bombing after Threats to End Gaza Coverage," *Middle East Eye*, October 6, 2024.
3. Benjamin Netanyahu, January 13, 2024.
4. Amal Dunqul, "The Last Words of Spartacus," in *The Complete Works* (1969; Beirut: Dar al-Shorouk, 2012), 83. My translation.
5. "Ministry of Prisoners: 36 Gazan Prisoners Die of Torture in Israeli Prisons," Palestinian Information Center, June 21, 2024.
6. Some lines in this chapter also appeared in Mohammed El-Kurd, "In Every Corner of Palestine, There Is a Story of Dispossession," *Nation*, March 30, 2022.
7. Portions of this passage appeared in Mohammed El-Kurd, "Reflections on the 75th Anniversary of a Nakba That Never Ended," *Nation*, May 15, 2023.
8. Ghassan Kanafani, *On Zionist Literature*, trans. Mahmoud Najib (1967; Oxford: Ebb Books, 2022), 1.
9. Kanafani, *On Zionist Literature*, 4.
10. Part of this passage previously appeared in Mohammed El-Kurd, "What Role Does Culture Play in Palestinian Liberation?" *Mondoweiss*, September 5, 2023. Bassel al-Araj's words, in Arabic, from a presentation hosted and recorded by Zedne Club, December 25, 2016. My translation.

9. "do you want to throw israelis into the sea?"

1. Mahdi Amel, "The Revolutionary War in Lebanon Is Our Universe," *Al-Tariq Magazine*, August 24, 1982.
2. HC Deb. (5th ser.) (18 Oct. 1973) (861) col. 462.
3. Robert Weltsch, "Mayhew Action Dropped," *AJR* [Association of Jewish Refugees] *Information* 31, no. 4 (April 1976).
4. Weltsch, "Mayhew Action Dropped," 3.
5. HC Deb. (5th ser.) (18 Oct. 1973) (861) col. 462.
6. Mahmoud Darwish, *Mural*, trans. John Berger and Rema Hammami (2000; New York: Verso, 2017), 54.
7. Darwish, *Mural*.
8. Mahmoud Darwish, *Unfortunately, It Was Paradise: Selected Poems*, ed. and trans. Munir Akash and Carolyn Forché (Oakland: University of California Press, 2003), 161.
9. *Middle East Eye* Staff, "War on Gaza: Netanyahu 'Suggests New US-Built Port Could Help Deport Palestinians,'" *Middle East Eye*, March 20, 2024.
10. May Golan, *Israel Daily*, ILTV News, February 21, 2024.

NOTES

11. Quoted in Noam Chomsky, *The Fateful Triangle: The United States, Israel and the Palestinians* (Boston: South End Press, 1983), 91.
12. To read more about Israeli myths, including "Israel Is Defending Itself," see Decolonize Palestine, https://decolonizepalestine.com/.
13. Emile Habiby, *The Secret Life of Saeed: The Pessoptimist*, trans. Salma K. Jayyusi and Trevor LeGassick (1974; Northampton, MA: Interlink Books, 2003), 25.
14. Steven Salaita, "The Importance of Being Flippant," *Mondoweiss*, May 9, 2022.
15. *New Arab* Staff, "Israeli Forces 'Poisoned Wells in Palestinian Villages' during 1948 Nakba, Unearthed Documents Show," *New Arab*, October 15, 2022.
16. Mohammed Najib, "Palestine Runs Dry: 'Our Water They Steal and Sell to Us,'" Al Jazeera, July 15, 2021.
17. Stephen Kekoa Miller, "The Importance of Not Being Earnest: The Role of Irreverence in Philosophy and Moral Education," *Metodički ogledi* 30, no. 2 (2019): 32.
18. For more information see "Myth: Palestinians Fake Israeli Atrocities," Decolonize Palestine.
19. Parts of this passage were previously published in Mohammed El-Kurd, "Alaa on My Mind," *Baffler*, December 7, 2022.

epilogue: rain is coming

A version of this text, titled "Rain Is Coming: The Ongoing Nakba and the Present Revolution," appeared as the cover story in the Nakba Day edition of *New York War Crimes* and in *Mondoweiss* on May 15, 2024.

Index

Abbas, Mahmoud, 103–5, 108, 178, 197
Abdalhamid, Kinnan, 119
Abdallah, Issam, 174
"Abd el-Hadi Fights a Superpower" (Ali), 79
"Abd el-Hadi the Fool" (Ali), 93–95
Absentee Property Law, 188
Abu Akleh, Shireen, 51–54, 56, 70, 73–76, 117
Abu Asab, Muhammad, 107
Abu Joas, Jamal, 47
Abu Khdeir, Mohammed, 11, 73, 75
Abu Khoruj, Othman, 107
Abu Salah family, 43
Abu Sitta, Salman, 161
Adalah, 162
Addameer, 162
Ahmad, Tahseen Ali, 119
Ali, Orwa Sheikh, 103, 107–8, 117
Ali, Taha Muhammad, 79, 93
Alnaouq, Ahmed, 80, 84–86, 88–91
Amanpour, Christiane, 67, 69
Amnesty International, 64, 160
Anti-Defamation League, 133
antisemitism, 103–6, 133, 154, 156, 159; disavowal of, 29, 80, 85, 89, 104–5, 114, 159, 161; tropes of, 101, 109, 203; victim status and, 92, 109–10
Al-Aqsa Mosque, 57, 76
Al-Aqsa Intifada, 147–48
Arabic language, 4, 21, 26, 44, 75, 190; Abd el-Hadi and, 79, 93–95; ajanib and, 14, 20, 34
Arafat, Yasser, 200

al-Araj, Bassel, 190
al-Areer, Refaat, 44
al-Aref, Aref, 161
Arna's Children (Mer-Khamis), 147
As'ad, Omar, 54–55, 73
Asfour, Tulin, 139
Atlantic, 71, 149
Australia, 17–18
Awartani, Hisham, 119–20
Ayyad, Adam, 40
Baghdad Bombings, 157
Bahr al-Baqar, 157
Bakir, Marah, 140–41
Bakr, Ahed, Ismail, Mohamed, and Zakaria, 149
Balat al-Shuhada Street, 52
Baldwin, James, 97, 143, 146
Banat, Nizar, 104–5, 178
Bangladesh, 144
Barghouti, Mourid, 85
Battle of Jenin, 147–48
BBC, 12–13, 111
Bedouins, 181
Beirut, 153, 180
Beita, 107, 181
Beit Hanina, 107, 140, 141
Beitin, 127
Beit Jala, 40
Beit Sira, 107
Ben-Gurion, David, 199
Ben-Gvir, Itamar, 107–8
Bet El, 127, 133
Bethlehem, 19, 40, 195
Al-Bireh City, 74
BDS, 47, 88, 126

240

INDEX

Breaking the Silence, 160
Bronner, Ethan, 72
Brooks, David, 72
B'Tselem, 161
Cairo, 106
CBS News, 151
Cemetery of Numbers, 9
Center for Constitutional Rights, 133
Césaire, Aimé, 90
CNN, 67, 134
Columbia Daily Spectator, 126–28
Columbia University, 88, 126
Columbus, Christopher, 89
Committee to Protect Journalists, 171
Corrie, Rachel, 54–55, 59
Council on American–Islamic Relations, 133
Damascus Gate, 76
Daqqa, Walid, 141–44, 196
Darwish, Mahmoud, 164
Declaration of Human Rights, 67
Deir Yassin massacre, 154
Dichter, Avi, 153
Doar, Zacharia, 119
Dunqul, Amal, 136, 178–79
Dura al-Qari', 127
Durra, 104
al-Durrah, Ahmad, 140
al-Durrah, Jamal, 140, 149
al-Durrah, Muhammad, 140, 149
Egypt, 193
Esmail, Samaher, 47
Europe, 11, 36, 65, 69, 103, 105–6, 109, 136, 175, 178
al-Fayoume, Wadea, 119
Financial Times, 68
First Intifada, 71, 93, 128
Freedom and Dignity List, 104
Freedom Theater, 47, 147
Friedman, David, 128
Galilee, 79, 102, 147
Gaza, 29, 58, 81, 91, 152, 177, 184, 190, 191; 1948 Nakba and, 61, 183,

211; genocide in, 2, 9, 12, 17, 43, 55, 67, 70–71, 80, 119, 121, 126, 140, 145, 151, 153, 158, 165, 168, 183–84, 197–98, 203, 211; Israeli assaults on, 182; journalists in, 70, 119, 145, 166; north of, 43, 111, 114, 119; Rachel Corrie murdered in, 54; resistance in, 44, 61, 140; siege of, 17, 128, 166, 182, 198, 211; south of, 9; *Times* coverage of genocide in, 64, 171; universities destroyed in, 203; water in, 8, 68. *See also* Great March of Return
Gaza City, 44
Geneva Conventions, 28, 60
Ghannam, Abdul Rahim Fayez, 107
Al-Ghawi family, 141
Gilboa prison, 148
"God Is a Refugee" (Hussein), 187
Golan Heights, 100, 182
Goldberg, Jeffrey, 71
Goldstein, Baruch, 108
Great March of Return, 99, 128
Greenberg, Joel, 72
Guardian, 63, 138
Haaretz, 160, 167
Haddad, Fouad, 75
Haganah, 182
Hagee, John, 156–57
Haifa, 62, 112, 182
Hamas, 12, 64–67, 69–70, 72, 112, 118, 122, 141, 153, 205
al-Hamdani, Abu Firas, 125
Hamdan, Rami, 142
Hammad, Nufooz, 141
Al-Haq, 162
Harlem, 143, 146
Hartman, Saidiya V., 101
Hebron, 53, 107, 108, 178
Hendel, Yoaz, 153
Herzl, Theodor, 154
Herzog, Isaac, 111–12, 118
Hezbollah, 125

242 PERFECT VICTIMS

Hitler, Adolf, 101, 112, 157
Holocaust, 101, 103, 114–15, 121, 155, 158, 203
Hospitals: Al-Ahli, 118; Al-Hussein, 40; Saint Joseph, 56, 75; Al-Shifa, 122
Human Rights Watch, 160
Hussein, Rashid, 62, 187
Ibrahimi Mosque, 108
Institute for National Security Studies (INSS), 71–72
Institute for Palestine Studies, 106
International Court of Justice, 3
International Press Freedom Awards, 171
International Solidarity Movement, 54
Ir Amim, 160
Iraq, 79, 131, 157
Irgun, 154
Irish Republican Army, 65
I Shall Not Hate (Abuelaish), 81, 83
Islam, 76
Islamic Jihad movement, 147
Islamic University of Gaza, 44
Islamophobia, 122, 126
Israel, 39, 65, 108, 127–28, 148, 152, 154, 180, 198–99, 202; airstrikes by, 12, 44, 58, 119; apartheid in, 158, 161; bombing of Palestine Research Center by, 106; bulldozers of, 54–55, 59; courts of, 26, 98–99, 181; flag, 99, 108; government of, 17, 21, 99, 102, 111, 115, 121, 131, 141, 153, 156, 197, 199; human rights organizations in, 155, 161; as "Jewish state," 98, 101, 102, 105; Land Law, 187; Lebanon invasion of (1982), 130, 157; *Mein Kampf* in, 119; Nation-State Law, 98–99; normalized relations with, 137; nuclear capabilities of, 69; police of, 75, 103, 107, 117, 131, 140–41, 178, 180, 208; Said on, 131; television in, 153; torture by, 8, 99, 114, 141; university investments and, 88; water used as weapon of war by, 8, 68

Israeli occupation forces (IOF), 71, 115–18, 120, 147, 182, 203; Break the Bones policy of, 130; ejected from Lebanon, 125; intelligence of, 76, 103; murder of Abu Salah family by, 43; murder of Arna's children by, 148; murder of children by, 12, 40, 81, 126, 140, 149, 151, 206; murder of Israeli hostages by, 43; murder of Jawad and Thafer Rimawi by, 62–63; murder of journalists by, 51–56, 59, 70, 74, 75, 117, 171–74, 191; murder of Mohammed Zubeidi, his grandmother, and his uncle by, 148; murder of Muhammad and Ahmad al-Durrah and their uncles by, 140; murder of Omar As'ad by, 54, 73; murder of protesters by, 99, 122; murder of Refaat al-Areer by, 44; murder of Thaer Yazouri by, 74; murder of Walid Sharif by, 57; *New York War Crimes* on, 64; Said's stone and, 128–30; shooting of Marah Bakir by, 140; shooting of Rami Srour by, 74; tanks of, 180, 208
Israeli Security Agency, 99
Al-Ittihad, 57
Jabotinsky, Vladimir, 154
Jaffa, 61, 183
Jaffa Gate, 75, 76
Jaffa Street, 136
Al-Jaghoub, Ameed, 107
Jamous, Lama, 145
Al Jazeera, 51–52, 56
Jenin, 51–52, 61, 74–75, 107, 144–45, 147–48
Jericho, 107, 145
Jerusalem, 11, 19, 52, 62, 97, 99, 108, 137, 139, 156, 178, 180, 195, 197; forced expulsions in, 26, 109, 136–37; funeral for Shireen Abu Akleh in, 56, 74–76; *Times* correspondents in, 71–72
Jerusalem Post, 160
Jewish Insider, 70

INDEX

Jewish National Fund (JNF), 78, 182
Jewish Voice for Peace, 133
Jihad, Janna, 145
Jiljilya, 54
journalism, 4, 24, 58, 70–74, 95, 168, 171–73; permission to narrate and, 134, 151, 157, 159, 168
Kanafani, Ghassan, 24, 48, 143, 188
Kashmir, 29
Kershner, Isabel, 71–72
Ketziot prison camp, 71
Khalil, Enas, 139
Khan Yunis, 180, 202
King David Hotel, 154
Knesset, 98, 106, 153, 198
El-Kurd, Maha, 139
El-Kurd, Rifqa, 33–34, 98, 101, 159, 182, 191, 203
Kushner, Jared, 128
Kuwait, 131
Lalu, Shahidul Islam, 144
Land and Afforestation Department, 78
Land Movement, 62
Land of Our Own, A (Meir), 116
Lebanon, 79, 125–26, 130, 139, 157, 174, 189
"Letter from a Region in My Mind" (Baldwin), 143, 146
London, 79–80, 84, 151, 180, 205
Lorde, Audre, 26
Los Angeles Times, 63
Makaber al-Arqam, 9
Makkawi, Sayyed, 75
Manasra, Ahmad, 140
Mandela, Nelson, 59
Masafer Yatta, 181, 182, 189
Mayhew, Christopher, 193
McCain, John, 138
Mediterranean Sea, 195, 198
Mein Kampf (Hitler), 111–14, 118
Meir, Golda, 116
Mema, Yousef, 119
MEMRI, 47, 103
Mereb, Ahed, 74

Mer-Khamis, Arna, 147
Mer-Khamis, Juliano, 147
Metropolitan police, 80, 205
Middle East, 65, 72, 81, 158
Milwidsky, Hanoch, 153
Morris, Benny, 160
Morrison, Toni, 153
Mousa, Ata Yasser Ata, 107
Movement for Black Lives, 133
Mukti Bahini, 144
Munich Security Conference, 112
Musta'ribeen, 75
Nablus, 75, 107
Nakba; of 1948, 33, 61–62, 78–79, 154, 157, 181–83, 188, 211, 213; ongoing, 11, 102, 151, 153, 157, 182–83, 195
Al-Naqab, 62, 181–82
Nasser, Gamal Abdel, 193
Nazareth, 79
Netanyahu, Benjamin, 115, 156–57, 197
Neturei Karta, 159
New York, 62, 139, 171, 180
New York Crimes, 64
New Yorker, 71
New York Post, 63, 112
New York Times, 56, 58, 63–65, 68, 71, 79, 118, 130, 167, 171–72
New York War Crimes, 64
Nofel, Islam, 107
Obaida, Abu, 92
Obama, Barack, 128, 138–39, 172
October 7, 2023, 12, 67, 80, 180, 185
Oil's Secret Tale, The (Daqqa), 141–42
Old City (Jerusalem), 20, 74, 102, 108
Olmert, Ehud, 154
Oslo accords, 178, 196
Othman, Orouba, 61
Pakistan, 144
Palestine, 3, 11, 21, 30, 58, 65, 70, 109, 145–47, 154, 156, 165–66, 183, 199; books about, 29, 160, 206; British occupation of, 24, 196; capitalism and, 162; cause of, 3, 41, 47, 136, 167, 187; flag of, 56, 75; future of, 88, 114,

244 PERFECT VICTIMS

195–96, 212; history of, 128, 168, 211; 1948-occupied, 75, 138, 188; US mobilizations for, 28, 88, 203
Palestine Research Center, 106
Palestinian Authority, 12, 103–5, 178–79
Palestinian Legislative Council, 105
Palestinian Ministry of Health, 56, 168
Palestinian resistance, 28, 40, 43, 47, 59–62, 66, 76, 154, 184, 188–90; academics on, 8, 15, 87; childhood and, 147–48; culture of, 24, 44; human shields and, 115; perfect victimhood and, 43, 48, 63, 151, 162; Said's stone and, 126, 130–31; termed "terrorism," 65–66, 115; *Times* on, 64–66. *See also* First Intifada; Great March of Return; Second Intifada; Unity Uprising
Palestinians, 4, 7, 16, 29, 53, 59, 86, 130, 156, 162, 185, 203; affective allowance of, 77–78, 84–85, 94, 122, 206; childhood and, 137–52; colonial projections on, 194–98, 202; commodification of, 163, 165, 167; conditional human rights for, 67–69; corpses of, 9, 56–57, 99, 107, 110, 119; crime of being, 51, 54, 74, 205; deemed either victims or terrorists, 21–23, 131–33, 162, 206; defanging of, 22–23, 38, 81, 137, 162, 164; dehumanization of, 13–14, 18, 46, 67–68, 151; demolition of homes of, 54, 62; in diaspora, 1, 3, 103, 107–8, 119, 165, 202, 205; dreams of, 195–96, 207; elite of, 46–47, 82, 165; ethnic cleansing of, 78, 121, 181, 197; eulogies for, 44–45; who are filmmakers, 163, 206; gatherings of, 75–76; in Gaza, 91, 119, 121; Herzog on, 112; humanization of, 35–39, 41, 48, 81–82; irreverence of, 206–9; Israeli courts and, 26, 99; Jabotinsky on, 154; who are journalists, 53, 59, 61, 70–72, 119, 145, 151, 157, 166, 205; Kanafani on, 24, 48; who are

martyrs, 3, 43, 55, 57–59, 64, 76, 109–10, 117, 119, 126, 139–40, 147, 168, 182, 190, 205–6, 209; who are men, 4–5, 43–44, 56, 62, 94, 103, 107, 114, 117, 151–52, 208 ; muzzle internalized by, 101, 118; not all Hamas, 12, 61, 65, 67, 69–70, 72, 205; open letter in defense of, 103–4; Palestinian Authority and, 104; permission to narrate of, 133–39, 152, 157, 159–69, 207; who are poets, 9, 14, 24, 163–64; who are prisoners, v, 3, 46, 53, 62, 108, 131, 140–44, 148, 153, 157, 176–77, 180, 186, 196; racial slur against, 131; scholarship on antisemitism by, 106; self-definition and, 20, 27; who are upwardly mobile, 46, 104, 132, 205; unity among, 75–76; value systems and, 89–90
Palestinian Youth Movement, 119
Pappé, Ilan, 160
Patel, Riddhi, 47
Perlmutter, Mark, 151
Pisgat Ze'ev, 141
politics of appeal, 2, 22, 24–29, 42, 47, 137, 160
Qabbani, Nizar, 9
Qalandiya checkpoint, 62, 139
Qalqilya, 107
Quran, 21, 26, 126
Rabin, Yitzhak, 128, 197
Rafah, 54, 117
Rajab, Hind, 11–12, 73
Ramadan, 57, 76
Ramallah, 54, 74, 75, 139, 177, 178
Ravid, Barak, 71
refugee camps: Al-Arroub, 57; Balata, 107; Dheisheh, 40; "Kuwaiti Peace," 117; Shatila, 157, 180; Shejaiya, 44; Tel al-Sultan, 117; Shu'fat, 103
Reporters Without Borders, 174
Reuters, 174
Revkin, Andrew, 72
Rice, Tamir, 142
Right Livelihood Award, 147

INDEX

Rimawi, Ru'a, Jawad and Thafer, 62–63
Rosh Pinna, 147
Russia, 63, 65
Al-Saadi, Bilal, 47
Saffuriyya, 79, 93
Said, Edward, 125–34, 152, 162
Sakakini, Khalil, 106
Salah al-Din Street, 83
Salaita, Steven, 202
Schumer, Chuck, 137
Second Intifada, 128, 140, 147, 182
Sha'ban, Yusef, 54
Sharif, Nader and Walid, 57
Sheikh Jarrah, 102, 107, 135–36,
    140–41, 159, 181, 183, 189
Sheta, Mustafa, 47
Shtayyeh, Mahfoutha, 189
Silwan, 102, 107, 181–82, 189
Sinjil, 139
Sister Outsider (Lorde), 26
Sky News, 63
Smotrich, Bezalel, 156
South Africa, 3, 154
Srour, Rami, 74
al-Sunbati, Riadh, 125
Syria, 100, 182
Taha, Raeda, 34
Tantura, 9, 155
Tel Aviv, 61, 115, 139, 176
Tel Aviv University, 112
Times of Israel, 160
Tobasi, Ahmed, 47
Torres Strait Islanders, 17
Trump, Donald, 128
Tubas, 107, 149
Tulkarem, 139
Ture, Kwame, 198
Turvey, Cassius, 142
UK Lawyers for Israel (UKLFI), 151
Ukraine, 63–65, 65, 156
United Kingdom, 11–12, 17, 24, 65, 84,
    111, 193
United Nations, 33, 44, 59, 162
United States, 11–12, 59, 65, 79,
    127–28, 133, 136, 139, 156–57, 172,

175, 197; Indigenous nations in, 89,
    154; mobilization for Palestine in, 28,
    88, 203; Palestinian Authority and,
    178–79; passport of, 52–55, 59, 74;
    racism of, 28, 35–36, 119, 172, 198
US Congress, 120, 136–37
Vaknin-Gil, Sima, 17
Warasneh, Ghofran, 53, 57, 59
War of Attrition, 157
Washington Post, 63, 126–27
We Are Not Numbers, 44
Weitz, Yosef, 78, 89
West Bank, 40, 51, 54, 75, 104, 108,
    120, 127, 149, 156, 178, 181
World Zionist Organization, 154
Writers Against the War on Gaza, 64
Yad Vashem, 159
Yazouri, Thaer, 74
Yesh Din, 160–61
al-Zaanin, Khaled Samer Fadel, 107
Zabane, Rania, 75
Al-Zaghal, Abd Amer, 107
al-Zahar, Mahmoud, 112
Zahlan, Rosemarie Janet Said, 162
Zionism, 11, 28, 65, 79–80, 99, 156–57,
    169, 176, 188, 190, 212; civilian
    status and, 61, 115, 117; as colo-
    nialism, 11, 106, 154, 156; colonial
    projections of, 194–99; dehumaniza-
    tion and, 42, 46, 151; distractions in
    service of, 121, 202; false claims in
    service of, 112–18, 120–21, 198, 203,
    212; forefathers of, 154–56, 168, 199;
    genocide as manifestation of, 91–92,
    203; ideology of, 11, 106, 116, 121,
    157, 181, 200; journalism of, 71–72,
    153–54; Judaism and, 97–99, 101–6,
    114. *See also* Nakba
Zionist organizations, 47, 127–28, 133,
    151–52, 154, 156–57, 160–61
Zubeidi, Mohammed and Zakaria, 148

about the author

Mohammed El-Kurd is a poet, writer, journalist, and organizer from Jerusalem, occupied Palestine. He is the *Nation's* first-ever Palestine Correspondent and an editor-at-large at *Mondoweiss*. In 2021, he was named one of the one hundred most influential people in the world by *TIME* magazine. El-Kurd is the recipient of numerous honors and awards and the author of the highly acclaimed poetry collection *Rifqa*, which has been translated into several languages. *Perfect Victims and the Politics of Appeal* is his nonfiction debut.